D0702199

Apples of Gold

APPLES OF GOLD

Voices from the Past that Speak to Us Now

M.E. Boyd

A word fitly spoken is like apples of gold in pictures of silver.

PROVERBS 25:11

BONNIE WALKER & ASSOCIATES
REHOBOTH BEACH, DE

Copyright©2019, 2020 by M. E. Boyd
All rights reserved.
Printed in the United States of America.
Revised First Edition
For permission to reproduce selections from this book
contact: info@MissConstitution.com
Cover by Wanda Jackson
Author Photo by Angie Moon
Book design by Bonnie Walker

All the public domain photos and portraits were obtained
from Wikipedia.net excepting Alexander Hamilton, Thomas
Paine and John Underhill from flickr.com, John Jay and John
Dickerson from creativecommons.org, Charles Woodstock
from people.smu.edu, and Gustavus Vassa and Marcus
Garvey found in picyl.com.

Printed in United States of America

To

William Bradford and his wife Dorothy

In courage there is often also despair

WITH MANY THANKS

to

Bonnie

Who really thinks about it

to

Helen

A study in courage and virtue

to

Roya and Peter

Why America exists

Contents

Preface

I want Americans to love their country, to understand how and why America came to be, to understand what is unique about her people, and how she can steer a positive course for the future with a clear eye. To understand how and why America came to be we want to place ourselves and our imaginations back in time. We can discover or rediscover the influences in any given period of varying philosophies, religion, and culture. We can observe the human behavioral threads that link all of us to each other over time immemorial.

In APPLES OF GOLD you will be introduced to different voices and differing views in specific periods of our history. You will be introduced to founding written expressions of proper governance as colonies of Great Britain and as an independent nation. You will be introduced to new concepts about what constitutes the laws that govern us; about the mysterious Doctrine of the Black Robe; about the puzzling Incorporation Doctrine. We will look at events, documents, and voices in the context of what the authors and speakers *knew and thought at the time* and what we know and think today.

As we look at our past, the consequences of some well-meaning decisions that created difficulties for our social order are unveiled. The common thread of human inclination that responds to certain motivators and is restrained by certain barriers has not really changed over time. With this insight, we might ask when making decisions for our country, whether we are unleashing the best or the worst of what we know about how people behave.

During our history our leaders have been both Mortar Minders and Change Agents. A Mortar Minder is primarily focused on stability, consequences, and experience; he or she embraces change with caution and examination. A Change Agent dreams of the possible and sees the now as an instrument for improving the past; contending, often, that consequences as a by-product of change are inevitable and can be handled adequately. A Mortar Minder knows how people are; a Change Agent is hopeful that they can be better. Both views are who we are as a people and both views are valuable and irreplaceable at any given point in time. The *irony* is that each of us holds both positions at the same time but emphasizes one over the other depending upon the issue.

Most Americans, in my view, are a combination of Mortar Minder and Change Agent. Very few are wholly one or the other. The people, the events, and the documents in APPLES OF GOLD reflect the irony of this dichotomy. William Bradford was a primitive Christian Mortar Minder with an eye toward the Old Testament of the Bible, strict adherence to the scriptures, and a realistic view about people. And yet he was also a Change Agent who courageously took his flock on a dangerous journey on the Mayflower to form a utopian community of simple Christian living believing that people can live communally and share equally.

By 1623, after three years of grievous want, William Bradford made a momentous decision. Instead of growing crops communally he allowed each family to have its own plot, to keep the food they raised for themselves, and share only the excess. And so, the Mortar Minder, William Bradford, became the Change Agent at that moment, and unknowingly unleashed one of the most potent economic principles of all time – the potency of self-interest in motivating human beings. The Scot Adam Smith would later refine this concept in his famous *Wealth of Nations*, published about the time of the Declaration of Independence, but the idea took root in the rocky and unfriendly soil of Plymouth, Massachusetts, one-hundred and fifty-three years earlier.

The founding documents of America and the voices long forgotten speaking to us now are the APPLES OF GOLD in the picture of silver that is America. Some documents and some voices lean toward change and some lean toward stability. Examining the tension between the two, examining the alienation it causes, can help us dilute the toxicity of our times and pull our country out of the current poisonous trap of our own making.

Introductory Thoughts

APPLES OF GOLD is divided into three parts that represent the three Latin sayings on the Great Seal of the United States designed primarily by Charles Thomson. *Novus Ordo Seclorum* (new order of the ages) begins with the new nation of America and its early founding documents, the Declaration of Independence, the Northwest Ordinance, and the United States Constitution. We explore just what this new order is and its embrace of part of the old order, including slavery.

The second part of the book, *Annuit Coeptis* (God favors our undertakings) takes us back to the earliest emigrants from Europe and their struggles to survive in their tiny enclaves along the Atlantic seaboard in conflict, sometimes, with peoples already here. The relationship with native-American tribes and individuals was complex and startling and tested the reality of existence with the tenets of faith. Part II takes us through our venture into imperialism and the advances of the Progressive movement at the turn of the 20th century.

The third part of the book, *E Pluribus Unum* (from many, one) identifies some of the aspects of American culture that provide unity for us as a people. Does the new order of the ages work today? Can the United States Constitution hold up in modern times?

This book is not comprehensive. There are many voices that should be heard on all the questions asked in this book and all questions that come to mind in reading it. Included are some relatively obscure voices that readers might not be familiar with and excluded are many well-known writers and leaders of their times. The book does not go past World War I simply because the decisions made by American leaders just prior to the Great War and the Great War itself have shaped, in my view, everything since that time and solutions for today's challenges

Apples of Gold

cannot be addressed sufficiently without a true understanding of the causes and impact of that war. We must first get to WWI.

APPLES OF GOLD represents a twirl on the surface of the ice, not a deep dive into the water. It is intended to give the reader a taste of the thinking and a taste of the times, not a study of the thinking and a study of the times. We face, as a country and as a culture, momentous decisions about our future so it is important and wise to take a look back at our past and reintroduce ourselves to the long-forgotten dreams and thoughts of the famous and not so famous. Each has a wisdom that can help us sync policy with what we know about human inclination for a more just and humane society.

Part I

NOVUS ORDO SECLORUM

New Order of the Ages

1

America Organizes and Prepares for Expansion

The hard-fought American Revolution has been won -- what to do next.

"It is well known that errors, either in opinion or practice, long entertained or indulged, are difficult to eradicate, and particularly so when they become, as it were, incorporated into the civil institutions and domestic economy of a whole people."[i]

JOHN JAY (1745-1829)

GOVERNOR OF NEW YORK AND

FIRST CHIEF JUSTICE OF THE UNITED STATES SUPREME COURT

We begin with the end of the beginning if not the beginning of the end. It is 1787 and we are a new nation huddled along the Atlantic seaboard as thirteen states, no longer thirteen British colonies protected by a great sea power and refined European state. Imagine the audacity of the American Revolution. Imagine the sheer luck or gift from God or both that drove a fortuitous wind and then fog that prevented the annihilation of Washington's troops in New York at the very beginning stages of the American Revolution. At some point in all our lives we have realized that we are alone as in a child that is used to a parent of some kind always there and now gone. It is a very frightening feeling. Here we were thirteen little states, newly freed from parental control, and now we must govern ourselves with little aid, with little help, and with little protection.

There must have been a large exhale from those Americans who signed the Declaration of Independence and then somehow survived the Revolution. What would a snapshot of America look like at this time?

Each state was characterized by a uniqueness of its social and economic foundations and its religious tendencies. Religion itself was the glue in the development of the West and the conviction of most American citizens in 1787 was manifested in some form in each colony. Some believed that the settling of America was the result of a covenant from God like the covenant delivered to Israel through Moses. More importantly, it was one of the "practices" that Jay speaks of that form an inter-generational civic institution of great significance. Each colony had various forms and sects of Christianity and favored one over the other. Some colonies were very tolerant of different forms of Christian practice and others not. Each person living at that time had memories of parents, grandparents, aunts and uncles, just as we do today, and each person living at that time had memories of belief systems espoused by the family or escape from belief systems the family abhorred.

They were used to a state church, but some felt strongly about a religious tolerance not known before. Most were very religious whether tolerant of other sets of beliefs or not. This in no way, so we don't confuse 1787 with today, meant that there was necessarily a tolerance of world religions or even atheism, only different ways of looking at the divinity or non-divinity of Christ and the worship and social practices associated with a particular sect. Most states at our national foundation had state-run and tax supported churches (New Hampshire, Massachusetts, Connecticut, Maryland, Virginia, North Carolina, South Carolina, and Georgia).

As important as religion was, and religion was very important in America in 1787, also important were the natural economic possibilities in each colony and then in each state. The South was agrarian. The South found crops that worked in its climate and crops that could be translated to cash as exports. Rice was the most important commodity, as was indigo, and its development as a crop brought together the engineering skills required to irrigate rice fields with the labor needed to plant, re-plant, and then harvest the crop. Northern economies did not have the extreme labor needs of the South and therefore developed a different set of commodities and a different social system around them. American wealth early on was founded on agriculture, as the industrial revolution was in its infancy, and the technological revolution did not even exist. When imagining 1787, think all things agrarian and what was needed to create a prosperous agrarian society. Also imagine slavery, its unrelenting nature, and its impact, not only on the people held, but on the people that did the holding.

Relative to the development of North America by Europe, one great invention was the compass. This invention is not a Western but an Eastern contribution and allowed the great explorers some degree of certainty that they might return to their home ports in one piece. All who made it home claimed vast amounts of North America for their nations under the International Law of Discovery, which meant that no other Christian Prince had declared the land his or hers.[ii]

Of equal importance relative to the development of agrarian wealth were survey tools and the notion of private property that goes with them. It is this notion of private property with legal boundaries and inheritable attributes that created an inter-generational continuity with wealth created, passed on, and compounded. The notion of owning private property instantly separated the societies of many indigenous inhabitants from their European counterparts. In addition, we skipped a feudal agrarian stage altogether. Each colonist who survived could own his or her own land.

So, there is our snapshot of America in 1787. It consisted of thirteen unique states with different economies that shared strong religious beliefs of whatever kind and took for granted the notion of private ownership and personal economic development. There was not yet a real national bond between these disparate states. Most felt loyalty to the state where they resided; relatively few felt a national loyalty to the new United States of America.

Among the unanswered questions were: How shall this new country be governed? Would Britain lick its wounds and return to conquer as the great and prideful power that it was?

The answer to governance was the creation of a United Nations of States entitled the Articles of Confederation.[iii] It was a confederation of states, each with one vote, each protecting its turf and agreeing to national interests only if no harm would come to its particular state. There was no provision in the Articles for a permanent chief executive; there was only a Congress. Just as each country in the United Nations has its own economy and its own social structure so, too, did each new state. Each state was used to fashioning its own agreements for imports and exports and running its business as it saw fit. These "practices" were difficult to overcome as they had been habits of the people for one-hundred and fifty years or more. Seven generations of certain assumptions and customs had created a good deal of prosperity and many citizens saw no reason to change anything.

Drafted by John Dickinson of Pennsylvania and Delaware in 1777 (one of the great lesser known heroes of our founding) and ratified in 1781, the Articles of Confederation was America's first constitution, a confederation of states in *perpetual* union. This would be important later.[iv]

Each state retained its sovereignty and its power not delegated to the United States. Full faith and credit were given between one state and another for records, judicial proceedings, and acts of legislation. Full ingress and egress were given between states, as well as all privileges and immunities. Each state, based on its own selection mechanism, appointed delegates to Congress annually, not less than two and not more than seven persons who could not serve more than three years.

Restrictions were relatively mild. States could not make treaties with foreign governments or keep ships of war unless authorized by Congress to do so. No state could declare war and must provide land forces as requested by Congress for common defense. Expenses were allocated among each state based on its land value and improvements. Disputes between states were settled by a commission of five judges selected or drawn from an approved list. Congress alone had the power to coin common money and to manage native-American affairs, but it did not have the power to tax individuals. It had the power to tax the state itself. When Congress was not in session, a committee of the states selected a

President to guide the affairs of state. Nine of thirteen state votes were required for almost anything. Canada was invited in but declined.

The question became *Can it work*? Can thirteen states with habits and practices hard to eradicate as Jay tells us, and jealously guarded at that, work as a team on behalf of the nation? Nine votes for most things, no incentives for compromise, our first Constitution provided limited time for even earnest persons to develop the skills of statecraft. The delegates of each state had pledged the inviolability of the Articles and a perpetual union under this constitution. What was to be done if it did not work?

Well, it did work to some extent. America was expanding. The British had secured from France the large tract of land in America's middle to the Mississippi River after the French and Indian War (1754-1763). With the scratch of a pen,[v] British colonial America became a huge entity. The British had tried to manage the growth as they had meager resources in North America, but settlement of this land began in earnest anyway. There was no stopping it. It should be noted and appreciated that Americans had the ability because of these vast holdings to simply move west. It had the feel, for many, of starting over. Perhaps a person did not do well in the East. Perhaps the tragedies of death and disease poured over a person's heart and soul and he or she had an opportunity to simply abandon and move on. Perhaps a man was demoralized by his lack of courage in battle or in protecting his family and just wanted a fresh start. This ability was not shared by many peoples at this time in the middle of the 18th century and it is one of the most important elements of the American experience.

Human beings are flawed. Human beings make grievous mistakes, many times with deep regret and shame and sometimes not. For a religious people, tragedy can sometimes feel like the hand of God is applying fairness or retribution. Americans, unlike so many others, had the ability to start over, to re-calibrate, to do better. This part of us has never gone away. The frontier is closed but the thought of re-calibration is always part of the American gut. Facing the Congress under the Articles of Confederation was the issue of the expanding Northwest Territory. This is the territory that later became the states of Ohio,

Indiana, Illinois, Michigan, and Wisconsin. How is the expansion of states in America to be handled?

First, native tribes and French Canadians lived in the Northwest Territory at this time. They could retain their customs and laws. For American settlers, provision was made for the descent and conveyance of real and personal property and the recording of wills. Governors were appointed and judges and other officers whose jobs included adopting and publishing civil transactions and transmitting them to Congress. Slowly but surely the structure of western civilization began to take shape in these lands. Legislatures were organized; laws were passed; militias were formed; private property duly recognized was protected; peace and good order were established within what we now understand as the Rule of Law.

What is the framework in our system for the Rule of Law? The American system is firmly based on the concept of division of authority and small units of community. From the beginning of settlement in the "new" world by the English, as well as the Dutch, physical territory was divided into counties and townships each with an authority over individual behavior that was thought workable and efficient considering human behavior. What does this mean? It means that people respond to boundaries that are closely associated with their physical existence. Those boundaries begin with parents and the organization of the family unit. The boundaries are extended to the community including schools and places of worship. They extend further into townships, counties, states, and lastly and *very lastly*, the national government. It was thought that the best way to assure peace and good order was to guide the individual where that person is most affected. We care what our parents think of us; we care what our teachers think of us; we care what our spiritual guides think of us; we care what our community thinks of us. As authority moves farther and farther away from a pressure that matters to a person, the less likely it is that a person will have respect for and obey the Rule of Law. This concept is at the heart of the American governing structure and system. It has been true since the early 17th century and was codified by the Northwest Ordinance in 1787.

America Organizes and Prepares for Expansion

The Ordinance outlined how a territorial legislature was to be formed and who was qualified to represent the inhabitants. It then outlined those fundamental principles that members of Congress under the Articles of Confederation thought important as framework for all civil law in the United States. It was clear to otherwise very disparate states at the very beginning of our nationhood, that certain concepts and assumptions undergirded our entire way of life in America. What did our first Congress think these concepts were?

1. No person shall ever be molested on account of his mode of worship or religious sentiments.
2. All inhabitants shall be entitled to the protections of the common law such as *habeas corpus*; trial by jury; appropriate bail; no cruel or unusual punishment; compensation for confiscation of property or services for the common good; the rights of property and private contract.
3. Religion, morality, and knowledge being necessary to good government and the happiness of mankind, schools and the means of education shall forever be encouraged.
4. Fair treatment of native-Americans guaranteed.
5. Equal footing of territories relative to the original thirteen states.
6. No slavery or involuntary servitude allowed although fugitive slaves could be returned to their lawful owners.

We can see the Northwest Ordinance reflected in the United States Constitution.[vi]

Article IV:

Full Faith and Credit shall be given in each State to the public Acts, Records, and judicial Proceedings of every other State. The Citizens of each State shall be entitled to all Privileges and Immunities of Citizens in the several States.

We can also see the Northwest Ordinance reflected in Article I:

The Privilege of the Writ of Habeas Corpus shall not be suspended, unless when in Cases of Rebellion or Invasion the Public Safety may require it. No State shall pass any law impairing the Obligation of Contracts.

And in the Bill of Rights:

Amendment I – *Congress shall make no law prohibiting the free exercise of religion.*

Amendment V – *nor shall private property be taken for public use, without just compensation.*

Amendment VI – *In all criminal prosecutions, the accused shall enjoy the right to a speedy and public trial, by an impartial jury of the State and jurisdiction wherein the crime shall have been committed.*

While the Northwest Ordinance is a great American document whose passage was very significant at the time, the assumptions, the concepts, the presumptions of the rights of human beings are very much colored by the British heritage Americans enjoyed and are very much a part of British common law and custom.

The British had experience over a long period of time about how human beings behave and what constitutes the best arrangements for peace and good order in British territories. Americans took these ideas and refined them considering the experience and geography of our expanding nation. It is 1787, and a new order has begun, although it has begun with all the errors of opinion and practice that were indulged in at the time and hard to eradicate, as Jay tells us. Alone now, we forged ahead.

2

We Substitute One Constitution for Another

**The Constitutional Convention of 1787; done in secret --
by whose authority?**

*"It appears to me there is an option still left to the United States of
America, that it is in their choice, and depends upon their conduct,
whether they will be respectable and prosperous, or contemptible and
miserable as a Nation. This is the time of their political probation, this
is the moment when the eyes of the whole World are turned upon them…
this is the favorable moment to give such a tone to our Federal
Government, as will enable it to answer the ends of its institution, or this
may be the ill-fated moment for relaxing the powers of the Union
exposing us to become the sport of European politics."[vii]*

GEORGE WASHINGTON (1732-1799)

A PORTION OF A LETTER TO THE STATES DATED 1783

The Articles of Confederation, however well-intended, were found
to be insufficient statecraft for the new nation. The Articles
functioned more like a league of sovereign powers rather than
adherents to one sovereign power, the government of the United
States. The new nation seemed particularly poised to be divided and
conquered by faction and by faction backed by foreign states. Who had
the ultimate authority? Whose hand would be seen by all as the hand that
mattered. In many families, at one time, there was the one final arbiter
of the direction of family life. Who would be that arbiter with thirteen
sovereign children each with different histories and interests? Who
would prevent one or the other from attempting to get a small advantage,
and multiplied, destroy the comity and unity of a national voice? These

were some of the many issues that arose and had to be dealt with under the Articles of Confederation.

It was hard getting money from each state for national needs; it was hard to get states to freely grant full faith and credit to their neighbors; it was hard to get citizens to think in larger terms than their immediate communities and states. In the most elementary sense, it was hard to get a quorum even to discuss national issues with travel so difficult and inconvenient. Leaders of the new nation grew concerned that we were at risk at a very fragile moment in our nationhood. Letters were exchanged; meetings held; certain leaders decided to meet in Philadelphia in May of 1787 and adopt a new constitution for the nation. What the Articles of Confederation had exposed, to those interested in the efficacy of the new nation, was the reality of human behavior and the tendency of human beings to fracture into interest groups, whether as debtors or creditors, whether as farmers or merchants, whether as Anglicans or Quakers, whether as Virginians or New Yorkers.

It was hot in Philadelphia that spring and summer and delegates from the states arrived in dribs and drabs. Rhode Island sent no one. The smallest of the states had no reason to think that her interests would be considered. James Madison arrived early with a plan in mind. The southern states were wary. Would their way of life be threatened? Would slavery be abolished?

This is one of those moments in history where some of the greatest minds and the most formidably talented persons all meet around large and important questions. Fortunately, George Washington agreed to attend and was immediately made president of the assembly. It is hard to overstate the impact the mere physical presence of George Washington had on all people -- his size, his carriage, his impeccable character.

Washington was well-liked by all people. Benjamin Franklin was also there, and the two men conveyed credence and gravitas to the whole proceeding. This meeting would be serious with serious people doing serious work. Pierce Butler from South Carolina moved that the proceedings be closed and that no discussion of the work of the convention be revealed.[viii] No one - not one single person broke his word.

We Substitute One Constitution for Another

Personal honor was a very valued commodity. One's word mattered. One's reputation was sacred. Of course, all these great and not so great men meeting in Philadelphia were human beings with all the characteristics of human beings. But, as sometimes happens in the inexplicable history of humanity, the whole was greater than the sum of the parts. Between May and September 17, 1787, they produced one of the most interesting and unique pieces of statecraft ever. But could it answer and correct the weaknesses and defects of the Articles of Confederation?

Like many of us who are working on a complex project, the delegates in Philadelphia began with the subject they liked and knew best — Article I which dealt with the legislative powers of the nation. They spent half of the entire four months on Article I alone. These delegates thought that Congress was the most important part of government because it represented the wishes and desires of the people through their elected representatives. Ever mindful of the tendency of human beings to faction and mob action, it was thought prudent to limit direct voting to representatives in the House of Representatives every two years. Representatives would be apportioned by population so if a dishonorable representative was chosen in a locality that person would only have an impact for two years. But that left the Senate of a bicameral legislative body and that became a discussion of great significance.

Virginia, Pennsylvania and Massachusetts were the big players. Shouldn't they have more influence? Would they not operate much as a "House of Lords" on behalf of the whole nation? The answer was a resounding "no." It was agreed in one of the great political compromises that each state would have the same representation in the Senate, two Senators, chosen by their state legislatures so that their state's interests, if not their sovereignty, would be adequately and properly represented in Congress. If not for this compromise, the entire proceeding might have disintegrated and the delegates on their way home where much personal business awaited them.[ix]

To understand the United States Constitution, we need be comfortable with *irony, with conflicting concepts*, with *mystery*, and we must also understand that the document is *inconsistent with some founding principles*. It was authored by the delegates to the Constitutional Convention of 1787 with certain delegates having more influence because of their talent, education, and personality than others. This would be true, of course, of any group at any time.

In the mission statement, or Preamble, these delegates state that it is the citizens who have the authority to ordain such a document not the delegates themselves. They are speaking for us; they anoint us with authority to ordain something; they represent what they think we feel.

"We (citizens) do ordain and establish." It feels like a vow. And just what did we ordain? We tell the world that we believe in justice (impartiality); that we want peace and good order; that we will fight for our sovereignty but will otherwise leave everyone alone; but most importantly we want to be left alone to grow and develop as individuals without being directed at every turn by government. We want our personal liberty and we want it for our children and our children's children.

This is a written document, (unlike Great Britain) a written governing document for the nation. It is not a set of platitudes; it is a structure with force; and it considers everything known at that time about how human beings behave. So, in a very real sense, it is about how to deal with faction, with betrayal, with mob action unrelated to facts, with those with and without power, with individual behavior, keeping in mind that the same flaws in citizens are present also in citizen's representatives. Put as simply as possible, the idea is if the statecraft of the nation is divided up into small pieces no breakdown of one of the pieces should destroy the entire structure. The broken part could be replaced and fixed and the whole could remain solid. It was never anticipated that the whole structure could be attacked and weakened at one time and possibly collapse. Think of the flawed kings and autocrats throughout history whose behavior, when malignant, destroyed whole societies. This would not happen with America, it was hoped.

One of the wonderful things about having children is that when one looks at a new baby one is awed by the fact that none of the mistakes usually made in life have been made yet. This person represents a new beginning. That is what it felt like in 1787 – a new beginning for humankind; a new beginning for the citizens of America; an enlightened and effective way to deal with the vagaries of human motivation and action.

Thomas Paine (1737-1809), in a widely printed pamphlet called "Common Sense" published in 1776, stated succinctly the need for government and why monarchies don't produce human happiness.

> *Here then is the origin and rise of government; namely, a mode rendered necessary by the inability of moral virtue to govern the world ... monarchy and succession have lain but the world in blood and ashes. Tis a form of government which the word of God bears testimony against, and blood will attend it.[x]*

With the colonial experience and history in mind, then, the framework for a new order for the ages began. Article I included the following provisions:

- Representatives must be at least 25 years old; senators must be at least 30 years old – there will be no infants or children who inherit seats of government.
- Congress will be paid for their services so that a citizen of any means may serve.
- Titles of nobility are forbidden – there is no patrician class by birth, only ability.
- No more hereditary rights, but there was still a need for virtuous and politically competent citizens in government.

The Founders looked for ways to thwart corruption and self-interest in the halls of national power and included provisions toward that end. Among those were:

- Legislation for raising revenue must begin in the House of Representatives as it is closest to the people and the people's money is being spent, in trust.
- Impeachment (accusation) of civil officers of the national government including the President begins in the House of

Representatives as the House represents the larger number of citizens.

- Trials for impeachment are conducted in the Senate with the Chief Justice of the Supreme Court presiding if the accused is the President. This is a political event not a legal event and the remedy for misconduct that would cause the Senate to convict by a two-thirds majority is removal from public service, i.e. a type of shame. When in trial the Senators would be under oath of personal honor to assure that their decision is honorable.

More importantly, to secure personal liberty for those living and their descendants, it was thought necessary to limit the scope of the federal government to named powers, limited and enumerated, and then give Congress the power to make all laws necessary and proper to carry out these powers. What are these powers specifically?

Congress would be allowed to:

- Borrow money backed by the credit of the nation
- Regulate commerce within the union, with other nations, and with native-American tribes
- Establish rules for naturalization and bankruptcy
- Coin money and establish standardized weights and measures
- Provide punishment for counterfeiting monies
- Establish Post Offices and national roads
- Establish patent and trademark protections
- Create lower courts than the Supreme Court
- Define and punish piracy and other international crimes
- Declare war; to hire private naval vessels for national use
- To create rules of warfare
- Raise and support an army for no more than two years (the Founders were fearful of a standing army)
- Provide and maintain a navy
- Create rules for the military

- Provide for training and discipline of the militia whose officers would come from the states, and to be able to call forth the militia when necessary against invasion or insurrection
- Have full authority over the seat of national government and, with permission of a state, purchase property for needful buildings associated with the national government

These powers, in the opinion of the Constitutional Convention members, and a taxing authority, gave enough vigor for a true national government. As the listed powers are limited, national power would not threaten the state's plenary responsibilities over its people. This "selling point" would be highly contested at the ratifying conventions by those opposed to the new constitution. The anti-Federalists, as they were called, thought the whole exercise illegitimate and that its taxing and commerce authority would ultimately result in power shifting to the federal government and away from the states. The Convention members were quite aware what can happen when vast amounts of money are combined with a powerful military. The creations of division of power between the states and the national government (Federalism) and separation of power between federal functions were the mechanisms for controlling this age-old problem of abuse and corruption. The boundaries of behavior closest to the individual were maintained through state, county, township, village, community, religious, and family authority, but the "tone to our federal government," as Washington called it, would be strong enough to thwart any "European political sport."

Whether national in character or more local or familiar in character adherence by the individual to the Rule of Law is a core component to our system. What do we mean when we say Rule of Law? We are talking about four bundles of law, quite separate, that constitute the Rule of Law we honor.

1. *Unwritten law* that represents the traditions and customs of a people – the manners of intercourse between individual people, courtesy, comity.
2. *Natural law* as reflected in the Declaration of Independence that all people are born equal relative to inherited aristocracy and that

people create government structures to assist them in protecting their lives and their property and that government serves these ends.

3. *Moral law* as reflected in what the society defines as right and wrong. In America our moral law is grounded in Judeo-Christian belief systems and the Greek notion of virtue.

4. *Positive law* is the codification of some unwritten, natural, and moral law and is represented in *written* constitutions (federal and state), statutes, common law (judicial decisions going back to colonial times and earlier English and then British law), ordinances, and administrative rules.

Article VI

This Constitution, and the Laws of the United States which shall be made in Pursuance thereof; and all Treaties made, or which shall be made, under the Authority of the United States, shall be the supreme Law of the Land; and the Judges in every State shall be bound thereby; any Thing in the Constitution or Laws of any State to the Contrary notwithstanding.

What this means is the United States Constitution represents the supreme *positive* law of the land. Unwritten, natural, and moral law are separate from positive law and require due adherence and obedience. No positive law, however fashioned, is superior to the necessity for courtesy, for the acknowledgement of life, liberty, and the lawful pursuit of happiness, for rightful and principled behavior based on the moral foundations of the nation. It is this concept that is the basis for conscientious objection to positive law, sometimes reflected in objection to military service.[xi]

So here is the elementary framework of the Constitutional Republic established in 1787. Political power rests with the people (not the States) – with the people's consent. The people of the United States agree by covenant to honor the new constitution in order to secure their safety and well-being. It is an agreement bound by honor, but just in case honor is not practiced, the system is engineered to discourage abuse and corruption. Individual liberty is elevated to the nearly sacred but constrained and modified by the bundles of law one has agreed to obey. Our national constitution guarantees personal liberty, but one agrees, voluntarily, to be obedient to the entire Rule of Law – this is one of the central *ironies* of our system. Each citizen is free but constrained at the same time.

Patrick Henry opposed the new United States Constitution on the grounds that the centralized national government would eventually usurp the rights of the citizens. Speaking to the Virginia ratifying convention in 1788, he said:

> *"The public mind, as well as my own, is extremely uneasy at the proposed change of government. What right had they to say, 'We the people'? Who authorized them to speak the language 'We the people' instead of 'We the states'? States are the soul of a confederation. I have the highest respect for the gentlemen who formed the Convention, but I would demand the cause of their conduct. That they exceeded their power is perfectly clear. [W]e are wandering on the great ocean of human affairs. We are running we know not whither. The Federal Convention ought to have amended the old system the object of their mission extended to no other consideration."*[xii]

What right did the Convention have to author a completely new system in secret over four months instead of amending the Articles of Confederation? To many it was a sinister plot. To George Washington it was a necessary step to ensure our prosperity and to also ensure that no European military power got the notion that we were impotent as a nation and therefore easily conquered.

The United States Constitution is all about process. By replacing rather than amending the Articles of Confederation, the Founders thought the end justified the means. This is one of the *ironies* of our founding and was hotly debated at the time. On opposite sides of the question, George Washington and his longtime friend George Mason rarely spoke again.

3

What to Do About Slavery

**All people have unalienable rights to life and liberty --
so how is slavery in America possible?**

*We have seen the mere distinction of color made in the most
enlightened time; a ground of the most oppressive dominion ever
exercised by man over man.''[xiii]*

JAMES MADISON (1751-1836)

AT THE CONSTITUTIONAL CONVENTION, 1787

James Jackson,[xiv] a United States Senator from Georgia, gave a speech in Congress in 1790 in favor of a motion to thwart an attempt by Quakers to end the slave trade. In a petition signed by 535 people, including Benjamin Franklin as President of the Pennsylvania Society for Abolition of Slavery, the Quakers submitted to the new Congress a plea to make consistent the principles of the Declaration of Independence with the United States Constitution. It was referred to a committee and the committee concluded that ending the slave trade "would be highly injurious to some states." Senator Jackson in his long speech went on to say that while an evil habit, in some situations that habit is necessary. What people, he went on, having engaged in the slavery have ever abolished it? Jackson felt that neither Judaism nor Christianity found slavery repugnant as he proved over and over with Biblical references.

Benjamin Franklin's satirical response was an essay which appeared in the *Federal Gazette* regarding the enslavement of Christians captured by Muslims. He quotes the fictitious Sidi Mehemet Ibrahim who also opposed a petition to end slavery and piracy in Algeria in 1687. Excerpts of his statement mirror the Senator's.

> *"If we cease our cruises against Christians, how shall we be furnished with the commodities their countries produce? If we forbear to make slaves of their people, who are to cultivate our lands? Is there not more compassion due us as [Muslims] than to those Christian dogs? If we cease taking and plundering the infidel ships and making slaves of the seamen and passengers, our lands will become of no value. Who is to indemnify their masters for their loss? Is our treasury sufficient? And if we set our slaves free what is to be done with them? They will not embrace our holy religion; they will not adopt our manners; our people will not pollute themselves by intermarrying with them. Men accustomed to slavery will not work for a livelihood when not compelled. God has given the world and all it contains to his faithful [Muslims], who are to enjoy it of right as fast as they conquer it. Let us hear no more of this detestable proposition, the manumission of Christian slaves, the adoption of which would, by depreciating our lands and houses, create universal discontent and provoke insurrections to the endangering of government and producing general confusion."*[xv]

What was crucial in the thinking of the authors of the Declaration of Independence, of the Northwest Ordinance, and of the United States Constitution in 1787, was that all persons are born equally free; that each person has rights from God that come with his or her humanity. How did they justify the slavery that existed in America, then? Was this one of the errors and habits that Jay spoke of?

The Founders couldn't justify it, but they felt they could not end the practice and create a new constitution for the United States. It would never receive the nine state votes necessary for ratification. So, they talked themselves into thinking that slavery was on its way out, that it was a dying institution and that saving the nation from "European sport" was a greater need.

What to Do About Slavery

Jefferson explains the dilemma in this way:

> *"Can the liberties of a nation be thought secure when we have removed their only firm basis, a conviction in the minds of the people that these liberties are of the gift of God? That they are not to be violated but with His wrath. Indeed, I tremble for my country when I reflect that God is just; I think a change already perceptible, since the origin of the present revolution. The spirit of the master is abating, that of the slave rising from the dust the way I hope preparing, under the auspices of heaven, for a total emancipation."*[xvi]

The next excerpt is from the autobiography of one of those slaves, Olaudab Equiano, later known as Gustavas Vassa. He was kidnapped in the 18th century from Nigeria at age eleven and sent to the West Indies as a slave. He became educated and thus told his story.

> *"O, ye nominal Christians! Might not an African ask you – Learned you this from your God, who says unto you, 'Do unto all men as you would men should do unto you'? Is it not enough that we are torn from our country and friends to toil for your luxury and lust of gain? Must every tender feeling be likewise sacrificed to your avarice? Are the dearest friends and relations, now rendered dearer by their separation from their kindred, still to be parted from each other, and thus prevented from cheering the gloom of slavery, with the small comfort of being together and mingling their sufferings and sorrows? Why are parents to lose their children, brothers their sisters, or husbands their wives? Surely, this is a new refinement in cruelty which, while it has not advantage to atone for it, thus aggravates distress and adds fresh horrors even to the wretchedness of slavery."*[xvii]

The idea of enslaving human beings in Colonial America was an odious decision by both the colonists and the British. Labor needs notwithstanding it represents a departure from the sincere beliefs associated with what the earliest colonists thought as a special relationship with God that the settling of America made possible. The hypocrisy of the decision cannot be overstated and any other injury to the many disparate groups that have experienced difficulties assimilating in this country does not compare. Slavery provided the labor required for much of the agrarian wealth in America and by the time of the American Revolution that wealth was palpable. So, the question arose in creating the current United States Constitution in 1787 to replace the Articles of Confederation – what do we do about slavery? The following is what was decided:

Article I, Section 2

Representatives shall be determined by adding to the whole number of free Persons, including those bound to Service for a Term of Years, and excluding Indians not taxed, three-fifths of all other persons.[xviii]

This part of Article I does not mean that slaves are considered less than a whole person as human beings. It means that for purposes of determining the number of representatives in Congress, slaves will not be counted completely. At this time slaves outnumbered white inhabitants in Virginia. Were slaves not counted at all, as they were not considered citizens, the white South would have had less representation in Congress. If slaves were counted as whole persons, then the South would have had a larger majority in Congress. This compromise, then, was intended to create representational parity of the plantation belt with the North in Congress.

Article I, Section 3

The Senate of the United States shall be composed of two Senators from each state, chosen by the Legislature thereof.

Article I Section 2 gave the South representational parity with the North in the House of Representatives and Section 2 gave the South representational parity in the Senate. Many state legislatures used the three-fifths ratio for apportionment within the state giving plantation representatives a greater majority in state legislatures whose votes were then cast for two Senators. The result was a powerful pro-slavery Congress of the United States. The slave trade could continue until 1808.

Article I, Section 9

The Migration or Importation of such Persons as any of the States now existing shall think proper to admit, shall not be prohibited by the Congress prior to the Year one thousand eight hundred and eight, but a Tax or duty may be imposed on such Importation, not exceeding ten dollars for each Person.

Article II, Section 1

Each State shall appoint, in such Manner as the Legislature thereof may direct, a Number of Electors, equal to the whole Number of Senators and Representatives to which the State may be entitled in the Congress.

The electors from each state make up the Electoral College the entity that selects the President of the United States. The Electoral College is an indirect method of electing a President and ensures that any candidate must campaign in all states and not just those with large populations. It is one of the most important and ingenious devices created by the Founders to make sure that no part of America is unrepresented in the selection of President and in policy decisions made by a sitting President. In 1787, the bias in representation in the House and Senate and in state legislatures assured that the electors would be sympathetic to the slave states and any President so elected with its electors would not try to end the practice. In addition to important representation by small or rural states relative to electing a President of the United States, the Electoral College early on gave extra power to the slave-holding states by adding population for representation purposes through the three-fifths rule.

Article II, Section 2
He (the President) shall have Power to appoint Ambassadors, other
public Ministers and Consuls, Judges of the Supreme Court, and all
other Officers of the United States.

These Presidential powers, exercised early in our country's history by Presidents who were sympathetic to the South, had tremendous influence long after the President's term, especially regarding members of the Supreme Court, who were routinely confirmed relative only to competence and qualification, and who held office during "good Behavior" for life.

Article III, Section 1

The judicial Power of the United States shall be vested in one
Supreme Court and in such Inferior Courts as the Congress may
from time to time ordain and establish.

Pro-South Congresses routinely created Courts and placed on the bench judges sympathetic to the slave states. These judges also served for life.

Article IV, Section 2

No Person held to Service of Labour in one State, under the Laws
thereof, escaping into another, shall, in Consequence of any Law or
Regulation therein, be discharged from such Service or Labour, but
shall be delivered up on Claim of the Party to whom such Service
or Labour may be due.

This provision reached all the way to the Northwest Territories where slavery had been barred by the Northwest Ordinance, passed as you will recall, under the Articles of Confederation, but not included in the new Constitution.

What to Do About Slavery

Article V
Provided that no Amendment which may be made prior to the Year
One thousand eight hundred and eight shall in any Manner affect
the first and fourth Clauses in the Ninth Section of the first Article.

Article I, Section 9 allowed the slave trade to continue until 1808 and this part of Article V says that while the United States Constitution can be amended, no amendment may be allowed regarding the date the slave trade was to end.

And so, relative to the existence of slavery in the new nation of the United States of America in 1787, it was supported directly to 1808 and indirectly through the three-fifths rule. Then it was made, in Article VI, the "supreme Law of the Land" and the "Judges in every State shall be bound thereby, and any Thing in the Constitution or Laws of any State to the Contrary notwithstanding." In addition, Article VI states that, "The Senators and Representatives before mentioned, and the Members of the several State Legislatures, and all executive and judicial Officers, both of the United States and of the several States, shall be bound by Oath or Affirmation, to support this Constitution."

As personal honor was very significant at this time (duals regarding honor were not unknown), an Oath to preserve, protect, and defend a constitution that supported slavery sealed its support for some time. It was not until 1860 that this "lock" on our national government was broken. Errors or practices long entertained, as John Jay tells us, are difficult to eradicate, and particularly so when they become part of the civic institutions of a whole people. His statement not only speaks to errors and practices of the past, but to errors and practices that might become part of the fabric of society at any time.

One of the differences between 1787 and today is that the document of statecraft created then to assure ratification was obvious in its pro-slavery sentiments. This decision by the Founders not only not to abolish slavery but to allow the slave trade to continue for twenty years was made with open eyes and represented to many of the delegates a moral compromise between slavery itself and the continuance of the nation. It was a very difficult decision for many and rejected by many, as well.

It took seventy-eight years to end slavery in America with the ratification of the 13th Amendment in 1865.

Neither slavery nor involuntary servitude shall exist within the United States, or any place subject to their jurisdiction. Congress shall have power to enforce this article by appropriate legislation.

Congress enforced this article through the Civil Rights Act of 1866, later codified as the 14th Amendment to the United States Constitution and ratified in 1868.

All persons born or naturalized in the United States and subject to the jurisdiction thereof are citizens of the United States and the State wherein they reside. No State shall make or enforce any law which shall abridge the privileges and immunities of citizens of the United States; nor shall any State deprive any person of life, liberty, or property without due process of law; nor deny to any person within its jurisdiction equal protection of the law.

The 14th Amendment ratified after the horrors of the Civil War, codified the moral foundations of due process and equal protection of the law and continues to be the most powerful national Constitutional weapon on behalf of society's notion of social justice at any given time. Notice that not just citizens are protected by the equal protection of the law clause – all persons within a state's jurisdiction are protected whether they are citizens or not.

Looping back, the checks on the United States Constitution itself, although it is by ratification in 1788, the Supreme Positive Law of the Land, and by oath supported, are the three other bundles of law that American citizens adhere to: moral, natural, and unwritten. What this assures us is that some kind of monitor prevails over any one document, however well-crafted, and the Amendments to that document, however well-crafted. This is also true of Supreme Court decisions or any other positive laws that conflict with the other bundles that constitute the Rule of Law in America. It is these rarely noted checks by 'We the People' that compensates for the "errors" and "practices" that can creep into the civic institutions of the nation. Slavery, and the social ramifications of slavery, is a most glaring yet illuminating example of this observation.

The fact is that in 1787 a grand and difficult bargain was made by intelligent, educated, often lofty men who proceeded to entrench slavery into the marrow of our nation. In many ways it is a brilliant piece of statecraft and represents some of the most idealistic visions of governance for humanity. But Patrick Henry wanted to know the details of this bargain, the "side deals" if you will. He wanted to know what dangers were so immediate that the entire confederation was replaced with what might become a tyrannical centralized system. We know the bargain by its results, in part, including the fact that ten of the first fifteen Presidents were slave owners; more than half of the first Supreme Court justices were slave owners; and a majority of the first Speakers of the House were slave-owner sympathizers.

What was accomplished by this grand bargain was a more potent and stable nation relative to international players as well as to individual states, but the bargain is certainly *inconsistent with some founding principles* and at least two bundles of our Rule of Law. Without it, various state interests and factions might have divided the nation beyond repair as each faction sought connections with foreign powers that enhanced their regional prosperity. We will never really know. The question is whether or not entwining slavery with our supreme positive law in 1787 has created an error in Americans that they cannot undo or whether the adherence to other Rules of Law as well as the eventual correction by war and Constitutional amendment is sufficient moral re-calibration.

4

The Bundle of Law Known as Natural Law

One of the philosophical pillars of our social order.

"No wonder there are many great difficulties in reforming an evil practice of this kind, which has got such deep root by length of time. This matter ought, doubtless, be attended to by the general assemblies, and continental and provincial congresses; and if they were as much united and engaged in devising way and means to set at liberty these injured slaves as they are to defend themselves from tyranny, it would soon be effected."[xix]

REVEREND SAMUEL HOPKINS (1721 – 1803),

IN A PIECE DIRECTED TO THE CONTINENTAL CONGRESS, 1776,

REGARDING THE SLAVERY AND ITS CONTINUANCE

AS INCONSISTENT WITH NATURAL LAW AND OTHER REVOLUTIONARY PRINCIPLES.

Reverend Samuel Hopkin's congregation in Rhode Island had many slave owners and Newport itself was a major center of slave trading. The practice was not confined to the South initially.

The Constitution of the United States, as we have said, is part of the bundle of positive law that is really a codification of some unwritten, moral, and natural law. The document, however, that codifies natural law in its basic essences is the Declaration of Independence (July 4, 1776).[xx]

When in the Course of human events, it becomes necessary for one people to dissolve the political bands which have connected them with another, and to assume among the powers of the earth, the separate and equal station to which the Laws of Nature and of Nature's God entitle them.

In Latin we refer to this as *jus natural* or the law that should order nations in addition to positive, moral, and unwritten law. It might be considered less encompassing than moral law in the West as moral law includes natural law. For Aristotle it was universal law or ageless law. What is that law?

For America, natural law probably mirrors the thinking of John Locke in that it is really God's law as understood by human beings through reason. This understanding was first articulated by St. Thomas Aquinas (1225-1274). God's law tells us that human beings have rights that correspond to a person's existence and are not dependent upon positive or codified law or unwritten law as we know it. John Dickinson, 1766, said, "Natural rights are created in us by the decrees in Providence, which establish the laws of our nature."[xxxi]

As reflected in our Declaration of Independence these rights are life, liberty, and the pursuit of happiness. This essentially Jeffersonian document arrived at the precise rights God wills us by combining the thinking of John Locke and Jean-Jacques Burlamaqui who felt that man strives for happiness and therefore one of the natural rights is the pursuit of happiness. Locke felt property was a natural right, as well.

We hold these truths to be self-evident, that all men are created equal, that they are endowed by their Creator with certain unalienable Rights that among these are Life, Liberty and the pursuit of happiness.

In attempting to understand and evaluate the premises of the American system, we would note the absolute belief that a God exists, and that God is the author of nature and therefore the author of natural rights. These rights belong to man as a birth-right and do not require an organized law to validate. In addition to our moral law, natural law would forbid slavery, for instance, as violating the right to liberty, among other things. All men are created equally free and these natural rights supersede the United States Constitution and any other positive law. The issue with natural law and the American system is that it has not been enforced in the same way that positive law is enforced with consequent loss of liberty or property for its violation. Its enforcement is based on the voluntary honor code of each citizen to obey unwritten, natural, and moral law whether enforced by power or not. One of the great questions in our society is how is each citizen to know about this honor code and these bundles of law that they have a covenant by history to honor?

From the notes of Justice William Cushing whose Massachusetts court convicted a man for assaulting a slave (1783):

> *"A different idea has taken place with the people of America, more favorable to the natural rights of mankind, and to that natural innate desire of liberty, which with heaven has inspired the entire human race. And upon this ground our constitution of government (the Commonwealth of Massachusetts) Sets out with declaring that all men are born free and equal – and that every subject is entitled to liberty, and to have it guarded by the laws, as well as life and property – and in short is totally repugnant to the idea of being born slaves."*[xxii]

The Declaration of Independence goes on to say:

> *That to secure these rights, Governments are instituted among Men, deriving their just powers from the consent of the governed, -- That when any Form of Government becomes destructive of these ends it is the Right of the People to alter or abolish it, and to institute new Government, laying its foundation on such principles and organizing its powers in such form, as to them shall seem most likely to affect their Safety and Happiness.*

Well, there you have it. Americans wished to be free of what they considered the tyranny of King George III and they wished to institute a new government based on the natural rights of man, unalienable (cannot be taken away by any government) that included the right to be free and equal under the law, to have life and property, and to secure happiness as each person sees happiness. The new government instituted was the Articles of Confederation of the States (1781) and then the United States Constitution (1787) that did not grant life and liberty to all persons and, in fact, perpetuated slavery in the United States and did not even end the slave trade until 1808. Every Founder was perfectly aware of what was proposed and what was ratified, and many hoped that their compromise with the Devil done in order to secure a viable nation, would go down by the weight of moral repugnance by the American people. Slavery did go down, eventually, but by a long, vicious, bloody, ruthless, and difficult Civil War (1860-1865).

The following is an appeal to America's conscience delivered as a Thanksgiving Proclamation by Abraham Lincoln in 1863.

"It is the duty of nations as well as of men to own their dependence upon the overruling power of God; to confess their sins and transgressions in humble sorrow, yet with assured hope that genuine repentance will lead to mercy and pardon; and to recognize the sublime truth, announced in the Holy Scriptures and proven by all history, that those nations are blessed whose God is the Lord. We know that by His divine law, nations, like individuals, are subject to punishments and chastisements in this world. May we not justly fear that the awful calamity of civil war which now desolates the land may be a punishment inflicted upon us for our presumptuous sins, to the needful end of our national reformation as a whole people?"[xxiii]

Natural law, then, if enforced, would have prevented slavery in the new United States of America. (Recall that the Northwest Ordinance did call for a ban on slavery in the new Northwest Territories.) Although natural law is not directly enforced, the basic premises of natural law are still a large part of the American psyche. Natural law emphasizes the individual and the individual's liberty to pursue happiness wrapped, of course, in duty and obedience to other positive, unwritten, and moral rules of law. These concepts can be traced back to the Stoics and certainly Cicero.

The natural law concept of liberty is codified in the express language of the Preamble to the United States Constitution and in the 13th

Amendment to the Constitution. It is implied in our right to free association.

The natural law right to life remains one of the most vexing questions of our time, especially when two or more lives are weighed in value, and a life or death decision is made. It also applies to appropriate punishment, military engagement, and assisted suicide, among other things. This interesting bundle of law intersects with moral law and the two parts of each become one great continuing question for society. What is it about human beings, that allows us to justify certain absolute opposites at the same time? This is the *inconsistency with founding principles* that, along with *irony*, must be recognized to understand the Constitution of the United States and the compromises made to bring it to life and to preserve, protect, and defend it now. The errors would be corrected over time.

5

Individual Liberty Versus Governmental Intrusion

Powerful governments are often at odds with individual liberty.

"James, by the Grace of God, King of England, Scotland, France, and Ireland, Defender of the Faith do for Us, Our Heirs, and Successors, declare that all and every of the persons being Our subjects shall have and enjoy all liberties, franchises, and immunities as if they had been abiding and born, within Our Realm of England or any of Our said dominions."[xxiv]

FROM THE CHARTER OF VIRGINIA, 1606,

ISSUED TO TWO CORPORATIONS

FOR THE PURPOSE OF EXPLORATORY EXPEDITIONS TO VIRGINIA.

NOTE THAT "VIRGINIA" EXTENDED TO MAINE AND TO THE PACIFIC OCEAN.

O f great concern in 1787 were the rights of the individual citizen against government power and abuse of that power now that the federal government would have taxing authority and oversight over interstate commerce. Who knows whether these powers would produce yet another governmental tyranny? Ratifying conventions for the proposed United States Constitution were full of cries for a Bill of Rights to prevent the misuse of national power that the American Revolution was fought to overcome.

A sampling from Melancton Smith of New York, speaking at the New York ratifying convention:

"It must be recollected that when this plan was first announced to the public its supporters cried it up as the most perfect production of human wisdom. The same men who held it almost perfect now admit it is very imperfect, that it is necessary it should be amended. The only question between us is simply this – Shall we accede to a bad Constitution under the uncertain prospect of getting it amended after we have received it, or shall we amend it before we adopt it? Common sense will point out which is the most rational, which is the most secure line of conduct."[xxv]

A rigorous defense of the proposed Constitution went out in the form of the *Federalist Papers* written by Alexander Hamilton, James Madison, and John Jay. They pointed out the personal rights protected against government power.

Article 1, Section 9

The Privilege of the Writ of Habeas Corpus shall not be suspended, unless when in Cases of Rebellion or Invasion the public Safety may require it.

No Bill of Attainder [a law passed to inflict punishment on an individual without a court proceeding] or ex post facto Law [a law passed after a criminal act not before] shall be passed.

No title of Nobility shall be granted by the United States.

Article III, Section 2

The trial of all crimes shall be by jury; and such Trial shall be held in the state where the crimes shall have been committed.

Article IV, Section 2

The Citizens of each state shall be entitled to all the Privileges and Immunities of Citizens in the several States.

Article VI:

No religious Test shall ever be required as a Qualification to any Office or public Trust under the United States.

Individual Liberty Versus Governmental Intrusion

Individual states were restricted separately in Article I, Section 10

No State shall pass any Bill of Attainder, ex post facto law, (notice Congress could not pass either of these in Section 9 above) or Law impairing the Obligation of Contracts, or grant any Title of Nobility (Notice that Congress could not grant any title either. See Section 9, Article I.)

However beautifully stated and crafted the proposed Constitution might be, "We the People" wanted protections of personal liberty relative to national power. A common sense and relatively literate public, grateful for the genius displayed at the Constitutional Convention and impressed with the justifications in the *Federalist Papers*, could sniff out unintended consequences of lofty rhetoric and writings instinctively. It was true in 1787 and it is true today.

Demands continued for a separate Bill of Rights persuading James Madison to be pro-active in promoting and supporting amendments to the proposed Constitution in order to prevent a second Convention from being called. Madison diffused the whole controversy by delivering, with the help of others, some of the greatest written statements of individual rights against government power, ever. It forever reminds us that *people have rights; states have power.*

Those demands of "We the People" were ratified in 1791 as the first ten Amendments to the United States Constitution.

Amendment I

Congress shall make no law respecting an establishment of religion, or prohibiting the free exercise thereof; or abridging the freedom of speech, or of the press; or the right of the people peaceably to assemble, and to petition the Government for a redress of grievances.

Amendment II

A well-regulated militia being necessary to the security of a free state, the right of the people to keep and bear Arms shall not be infringed.

Amendment III

> *No Soldier shall, in time of peace be quartered in any house, without the consent of the Owner, nor in time of war, but in a manner to be prescribed by law.*

Amendment IV

> *The right of the people to be secure in their persons, houses, papers and effects, against unreasonable searches and seizures, shall not be violated, and no Warrants shall issue, but upon probable cause, supported by Oath or affirmation, and particularly describing the place to be searched, and the persons or things to be seized.*

Amendment V

> *No person shall be held to answer for a capital, or otherwise infamous crime, unless on a presentment or indictment of a Grand Jury, except in cases arising in the land or naval forces, or in the Militia, when in actual service in time of War or public danger; nor shall any person be subject for the same offense to be twice put in jeopardy of life and limb; nor shall be compelled in any criminal case to be a witness against himself, nor be deprived of life, liberty, or property, without due process of law; nor shall private property be taken for public use, without just compensation.*

Amendment VI

> *In all criminal prosecutions, the accused shall enjoy the right to a speedy and public trial, by an impartial jury of the Sate and district wherein the crime shall have been committed, which district shall have been previously ascertained by law, and to be informed of the nature and cause of the accusation; to be confronted with the witnesses against him; to have compulsory process for obtaining witnesses in his favor, and to have the assistance of counsel for his defense.*

Amendment VII

> *In Suits at common law, where the value in controversy shall exceed twenty dollars, the right of trial by jury shall be preserved, and no*

fact tried by a jury, shall be otherwise re-examined in any Court of the United States, than according to the rules of the common law.

Amendment VIII

Excessive bail shall not be required, nor excessive fines imposed, nor cruel and unusual punishments inflicted.

Amendment IX

The enumeration in the Constitution, of certain rights, shall not be construed to deny or disparage others retained by the people.

Amendment X

The powers not delegated to the United States by the Constitution, nor prohibited by it to the States, are reserved to the States respectively, or to the people.

Even today, these provisions seem very personal and were personal to Americans at that time. Two of them discuss a person's house and the inviolate rights one has in one's own "castle." Two of them discuss a person's right to be judged by other people just like themselves instead of simply being hauled up or away and out of sight by the arm of the government. "If I am guilty of something let my neighbors, who have similar lives, judge and punish me. No star chambers, no racks, no tortured confessions against my own person to satisfy the needs of the government for a 'legitimate' prosecution. Let me believe or not believe and worship as I see fit and allow me to bring to the attention of the government wrongs in society as I see them." Amendment X re-affirms the sovereignty of the people.

We, as the Sovereign, need an investigatory press to dig up facts to present to us and to uncover any corruption in the public sector. A free press is our eyes and ears. Finally, two of the ten amendments address both rights and power. Rights belong to a person; power belongs to the state. Both are residually retained by the Sovereign, "We the People", and we will hold all to account for misuse of power and denial of rights.

The Bill of Rights is such a powerful piece of literature that any opposition to the proposed federal constitution was whittled away just enough for it to be ratified. We shall discuss these rights further. In 1787, they represented rights against the federal government only and did not apply to the individual states.[xxvi]

Today, having extended some of the Bill of Rights to the states through a judicially created and still *mysterious* Incorporation Doctrine, our rights are protected by any state actor, meaning any arm of the government whether federal, state, or local and any entities that are "public" in that they are financed by taxes. The Bill of Rights does not apply to private entities, such as a private employer or other private organization.

Just so we don't forget; magnificent as this was in the history of humankind, it did not apply to the slaves then living in the United States. What was basically an acceptance of slavery as represented in the United States Constitution, as proposed, was ratified because of the attachment of a Bill of Rights, thereby obfuscating the underlying moral and natural law problem with the proposed Constitution itself.

The concept of governments being at odds with personal liberty is represented by our early governmental acceptance of slavery in a "free" society and continues to this day to be the ongoing leading tension in the relationship between the citizen and his or her government. Anyone who has been targeted and destroyed or damaged unfairly by an agency of the federal or state government knows firsthand what the sting of tyranny feels like.

6

Postponed Parts

The difficult Constitutional issues of the Presidency and the Judiciary.

"A feeble executive implies a feeble execution of the government. A feeble execution is but another phrase for a bad execution; and a government ill executed, whatever it may be in theory, and must be, in practice, a bad government."[xxvii]

ALEXANDER HAMILTON, (1757-1804) *FEDERALIST PAPER #70*

We are back in Philadelphia in that hot, hot summer of 1787, in a building sealed off from prying eyes and ears. The delegates are looking forward to a break in the proceedings toward the end of July. All the delegates' energies have been spent on the jewel of the republic, namely Congress, and the compromises that have been proposed and debated between the large and small states and the south and the north. They are all exhausted.

But what are we to do with the Presidency? Perhaps we should call him His Most High Excellency – no that won't do; perhaps His Most Luminous and Highest Excellency Ever – even worse. We are a republic; "Mr. President" will have to do. And that is about as far as they had gotten about the time of their summer recess. Various recommendations had been made such as allowing Congress to select the President or having a direct vote for President. The suggested term lengths included a single eleven-year term and a three-headed Presidency with one from each region. The delegates offered numerous ideas and made many speeches about the horrors of monarchy and tyranny of a too powerful a symbol in the person of the chief executive.

There were two other issues that added context to the discussion of America's chief executive: one was that the first President was sitting right there in their midst and it was a bit awkward to talk about this issue in front of him. Everyone knew George Washington would be the first and were very relieved to have someone that all agreed was impeccable of character to take on this new frontier. The other was that there was no example they could look to for guidance on what the optimum Chief Executive might look like and what powers he should and should not have. They appointed a committee to work on this issue.

Fortunately for our country the Committee on Postponed Parts was richly cast. Among its members were John Dickinson of Delaware, James Madison of Virginia, Gouverneur Morris of Pennsylvania, and its chair David Brearly of New Jersey. They met all through the recess and finally reported to the Convention in early September.

It is hard to appreciate today how difficult it was for these delegates to deal with one of the main reasons why the Articles of Confederation were scrapped for an entirely new governing document. Without a vigorous chief executive, no organization can function effectively. But how much power is too much power? The history of humankind is replete with takeovers of power by once benevolent rulers. It was a real dilemma. Finally, it was decided that the safest path was to let Congress select the President because Congress would be familiar with the possible candidates whereas the general population by might not.

John Dickinson, sick for most of the convention with severe migraines, persuaded his committee mates that the people themselves must have a say in the selection of President or they would not accept the Constitution at all. Dickinson was respected; he was moderate; he was cautious. He had not signed the Declaration of Independence precisely because he thought the colonies insufficiently prepared for the wrath of the superior British. For this reason alone, he has been left out of many conversations about the Founders when, in fact, he was one of the most important minds of them all.

But how shall the public participate? Unfettered and direct democracy scared many of the leading intellects of the day. They had just been through Shays' rebellion – almost a year's worth of civil unrest in Massachusetts over hard currency and debt collection caused by the Revolution that the federal government was unable to deal with. Mobs, sedition, violence by the common citizen all caused real concern to those delegates who had just lived through it and had seen its ferocity.

The Committee on Postponed Parts decided to accept James Wilson's idea of having an Electoral College select the President as a way of having the public participation that John Dickinson thought essential but avoiding a direct popular vote. The Electoral College is one of the most inventive and convoluted of the ideas that came out of the Convention and might be an ingenious way of compromise with the various factions of the Convention. The original version did not quite work so it was changed by the 12th Amendment, providing for separate balloting for the President and Vice President.

What is its purpose? Well, it was thought that the public could not possibly know the candidates thoroughly so that each state would select "electors" who would know the leading statesmen and could make an intelligent decision about such an important position. This method kept the states involved and that was a big issue in 1787. It also gave some small measure of equality between the large and the small states so that the more populous states could not just swamp the election with a numerical majority. It has resulted in some interesting situations when a candidate won the popular vote but not the electoral-college vote and therefore lost the Presidency.

Today it requires a candidate to campaign in all states for votes. So concerned were the delegates regarding direct voting that only one segment of the federal government was directly elected – the House of Representatives and they for only two-year terms. Even then the thinking was that the "smart" (think merit-based aristocracy) people were better positioned to know the persons and know the issues and be able to make an intelligent and reasoned selection of such an important post. In any regard, hereditary monarchy was rejected.

The hardest of issues – the Presidency – was left to a small committee while the rest of the delegates rested or went home. George Washington went fishing.[xxviii]

Article II, Section 1

The executive Power shall be vested in a President of the United States of America.

This was different wording than in Article I, which vested Congress with legislative power *herein granted.* Did it mean that the President did not have power unless it was specifically *granted* in Article II or did it mean that the President had plenary power unless specifically *restricted*? Perhaps the Committee of Style did not notice this slight variation, but it has been left to each President to interpret it based on his predilection regarding power. Theodore Roosevelt thought the latter and William Howard Taft thought the former.

Article II, Section 3

He shall take care that the laws be faithfully executed.

These are the laws passed by Congress and what "faithfully executed" means to each President is very individual. Some ignore laws they do not like; some impound funds for laws they do not like and some honor laws they do not like. A great question for a Presidential candidate: How does one interpret *faithfully execute*? Much of the power of the Presidency as originally conceived by delegate Brearly's committee is shared with the Senate. The President can make treaties with the Senate's advice and consent; he can appoint public ministers and officers of the United States with their advice and consent; he can name Supreme Court justices with their advice and consent. This was an important check on Presidential power thought necessary to thwart ignoble ambition.

Article II, Section 2

The President shall be Commander in Chief of the Army and Navy of the United States, and of the Militia of the several States, when called into the actual Service of the United States.

Postponed Parts

Everyone had George Washington in mind for President. He had relinquished rather than aggrandized his power. Surely this would be the example all would follow.

Article II, Section 1

> *Before he enters on the Execution of his Office, he shall take the following Oath or Affirmation: "I do solemnly swear (or affirm) that I will faithfully execute the Office of President of the United States, and will to the best of my Ability, preserve, protect and defend the Constitution of the United States."*

Well, here it is, *a President's role is not to protect the United States itself but the Constitution of the United States.* What is the difference? The difference is that the Constitution is a restrictive document. A President takes an oath to restrict his or her own power and to accede to other branches of government, not the executive, where that branch has authority. I vow to restrain myself, and to respect shared authority, so help me God.

David Brearly, as Chair of the Committee on Postponed Parts, read his report to the returned delegates on September 4, 1787. The Convention had only thirteen days left. The thorny issue of the Presidency had been crafted by a very talented committee. Those on the committee were not sure what the actual experience would turn out to be with the very short Article II. No doubt many fingers were crossed that all would be well. George Washington would fill in the blanks.

One more issue was left. What about the federal judiciary – Article III? Do we really need two separate and parallel court systems? Our colonial and now state courts are surely enough with perhaps the addition of one Supreme Court for national issues.

> *"To avoid an arbitrary discretion in the courts, it is indispensable that they should be bound down by strict rules and precedents which serve to define and point out their duty in every particular case that comes before them; and it will readily be conceived from the variety of controversies which grow out of the folly and wickedness of*

mankind that the records of those precedents must unavoidably swell to a very considerable bulk and must demand long and laborious study to acquire a competent knowledge of them. Hence it is that there can be but few men in the society who will have sufficient skill in the laws to qualify them for the stations of judges. And making the proper deductions for the ordinary depravity of human nature, the number must be still smaller of those who unite the requisite integrity with the requisite knowledge."[xxix]

ALEXANDER HAMILTON -- FEDERALIST #78

Hamilton reminds us of the view of John Locke – we must educate equally for character and general intelligence. Does this litany about the ordinary depravity of human nature apply to justices on our highest court? Are they, too, part of the folly and wickedness of humankind? If so, how can the Republic survive their partisanship, their improper motives, their lazy attention to the wisdom of the ages that has been accumulating in the British, colonial, and state court systems that might guide them to wise decisions? Can they not adhere to process not results? Can they stand being unheralded? The Founders found themselves left with *mystery*, not reason, the Enlightenment notwithstanding. This *mystery* is what I call the *Doctrine of the Black Robe.*

Article III, Section 1

The judicial Power of the United States, shall be vested in one Supreme Court, and in such inferior courts as the Congress may from time to time ordain and establish. The Judges, both of the Supreme and inferior Courts shall hold their offices during good Behaviour

One Court was authorized by Congress who may or may not establish inferior Courts. Notice unlike Articles I and II, no qualifications are described, nor is the Supreme Court allowed to establish its own rules and procedures. The Court was to have original and appellate jurisdiction with such exceptions and such regulations as Congress shall make. If a crime is committed outside of a state, Congress may direct where the trial will be held. So here was the device to check the power of lifetime appointments to the Court where, no matter how hard the system tries, one of the depraved, wicked, and foolish of humanity might take his or her seat on the highest Court in the land. The President appoints with the advice and consent of the Senate, and Congress oversees the creation, if it wants to, of an independent federal court system. It did so in the first Congress with the Judiciary Act of 1789. A President has limited appointments as he or she can only have two terms thanks to Amendment XXII, 1951.

We are still left with the possibility of politically motivated persons of inferior character and questionable intellect with lifetime positions on the Supreme Court of the United States. The ultimate check is the transformation that takes place in the robing room of all Courts. It is the *Doctrine of the Black Robe*. A judge or justice comes to Court as a regular citizen, full of opinion and ambition, but transforms with the donning of the robe of authority into the circumspect, neutral, process-oriented jurist that assures the stability and continuity of governance in the Republic.

Without this *mystery*, with its restraining effects on temperament, a Supreme Court justice or any other justice might simply reflect the political views of the person who appointed him or her and not step away from that loyalty to loyalty to the body politic as a whole. It is Article III where the Enlightenment and Romanticism meet, join hands, and ultimately decide what the Supreme Positive Law of the Land is.

What was, in some ways, the stepchild of the Constitutional system created that summer, has now become the one almost universally respected branch that is at once political, with all that the word "political" means, and at once non-political and almost spiritual.

In his prescient treatise on America published in 1831 and 1840, Alexis de Tocqueville writes:

> *"The peace, prosperity, and the very existence of the Union rest continually in the hands of these judges. Without them the Constitution would be dead letter; it is to them that the executive appeals to resist the encroachments of the legislative body, the*

legislature to defend itself against the assaults of the executive, the Union to make the states obey it, the States to rebuff the exaggerated pretensions of the Union, public interest against private interest, the spirit of conservation against democratic instability. Their power is immense, but it is power springing from opinion. They are all-powerful so long as the people continue to obey the law; they can do nothing when they scorn it. Now, of all powers, that of opinion is hardest to use, for it is impossible to say exactly where its limits come. Often it is as dangerous to lag behind as to outstrip it."[xxx]

The delegates were ready to finish up and go home. George Washington was especially homesick. The whole mess had been sent to the Committee of Style to be put into final form with the addition of a second way to amend the Constitution in Article V. As it happened, this mechanism has resulted in twenty-seven amendments to the Federal Constitution so far. A motion for a second Convention was rejected. There were grumblings and three of the remaining delegates refused to sign.

As Gouverneur Morris of Pennsylvania, the stylist of our Constitution quipped:

"I not only took it (the Constitution) as a man does his wife, for better or worse, but what few men do, with their wives. I took it knowing all its bad qualities."[xxxi]

In a generous gesture to the strong opinions and egos of the participants, Gouverneur Morris, in Article VII, states that the Constitution of the United States was "done in Convention by the Unanimous Consent of the States" rather than the individual views of the participants. It was thought that it would be easier for those with strong dissenting opinions to accept the document. They all lined up by state to sign and then retreated to City Tavern to enjoy the moment and prepare to finally go home.

If you close your eyes, can you see and feel what it was like in 1787? What it must have been like to participate in one of the great moments in history? Can you smell the fresh-baked bread and the lingering chimney smoke and the breath of the horses? We created a Republic that summer, if, as Benjamin Franklin warned, we can keep it.[xxxii]

John Jay – 1745-1829. Governor of New York; 1ˢᵗ Chief Justice of the Supreme Court; co-author of the Federalist Papers; founder of the New York Manumission Society. He also negotiated in 1795, with Washington's instructions, the Jay Treaty, which bought time for the new Republic in what was bound to be a second war with Great Britain. That war came in 1812.

John Dickinson – 1732-1808. Represented both Pennsylvania and Delaware. Known for his integrity and caution he tried to negotiate with George III of Great Britain on behalf of the colonies. When that failed, and the Revolution won, he drafted America's first Constitution – the Articles of Confederation.

George Washington – 1732-1799. First in war, first in peace, first in the hearts of his countrymen. America would not exist without him. Buried at Mount Vernon with his wife Martha. He valued and adhered to the United States Constitution as the first President of the United States.

Thomas Paine – 1737-1809. His pamphlet, *Common Sense,* made the case for revolution by the American colonies. It was widely read and extremely influential in turning a generally loyal public against Great Britain.

Patrick Henry – 1736-1799. Revolutionary War orator and twice Governor of Virginia. He opposed ratification of the United States Constitution as he was concerned that the power of the national government would eventually usurp that of the states.

James Madison – 1751-1836. Note taker at the Constitutional Convention of 1787 and leading proponent for the ratification of the United States Constitution and the Bill of Rights. Primary author of the Federalist Papers along with Alexander Hamilton. Was President when the British attacked Washington, DC and burned the White House. He and his wife Dolly escaped with prized paintings.

GUSTAVUS VASSA.

Thomas Jefferson – 1743-1826. One of the leading American intellectuals of his day and principal author of the Declaration of Independence. Governor of Virginia during the Revolutionary War; Vice-President and President of the United States. Jefferson sold his extensive book collection to the United States for the Library of Congress.

Gustavas Vassa – 1745-1797. Olauda Equiano from Nigeria. Enslaved as a child he earned his freedom and lived in Britain. He was part of the Sons of Africa abolitionist movement there.

Samuel Hopkins – 1721-1803. Calvinist theologian; Yale Doctor of Divinity, 1802. Ardent abolitionist credited with steering the Congregational Church into disavowing slavery.

William Cushing – 1732-1810. Long-serving Associate Justice of the original United States Supreme Court. While Chief Justice of the Massachusetts Supreme Court he asserted that slavery should be banned.

Abraham Lincoln – 1809-1865. First among American Presidents; he won the Electoral College but not the popular vote. Great thinker and writer. Never went to school. President during the American Civil War. Lincoln had four sons he loved dearly; only his oldest survived to adulthood. He and Mary Todd were extremely lenient parents.

Melancton Smith – 1744-1798. Anti-federalist from New York who eventually voted to ratify the United States Constitution of 1787.

Alexander Hamilton – 1757-1804. A Caribbean orphan sent to America by his benefactor. Founder of America's financial system; 1ˢᵗ Secretary of the Treasury; principal author of the Federalist Papers; trusted by George Washington and opposed by Thomas Jefferson. He died in a duel with Aaron Burr after refusing to apologize for a comment he had made about Burr at a dinner party.

Alexis de Tocqueville – 1805-1859. French writer whose visit to America and subsequent work, *Democracy in America,* is considered a classic study of American culture.

Gouverneur Morris – 1752-1816. Took the ideas of the Constitutional Convention and created the language of the United States Constitution. The Preamble is considered particularly eloquent.

Benjamin Franklin – 1706-1790. Recognized world-wide as a statesman, scientist, inventor, writer, printer, civic organizer (American Philosophical Society), and abolitionist. Founder of the University of Pennsylvania, and along with George Washington, indispensable at the Constitutional Convention in Philadelphia in 1787. A great humorist.

John Winthrop – 1588-1649. Distinguished leader of the Massachusetts Bay Colony. He envisioned a Puritan "city upon a hill" governed by virtuous religious leaders.

John Robinson – 1576-1625. Leader of the English Separatists and pastor to the Pilgrims. He never came to America but encouraged his flock to come and create a communal Christian enclave.

William Bradford – 1590-1657. Led the Pilgrims from Holland to America on the Mayflower in 1620. He lived in peace with the native-Americans, tried to keep his flock together in a Christian utopia; and lamented that many wandered from the community and his ideal.

John Underhill – 1597-1672. Head of the Massachusetts Bay Colony militia. He led the attack against native-Americans in the Pequot War of 1636.

John Cotton – 1585-1652. Leading writer and theologian of the Massachusetts Bay Colony. He labeled his theological position "Congregationalism."

George Hoar – 1826-1904. Senator from Massachusetts; ardent anti-imperialist. He opposed the annexation of Hawaii; the Spanish-American War; and the take-over of the Philippines by America. He is responsible for the return to the United States of William Bradford's *Of Plymouth Plantation* that had been stolen by a British soldier.

Elizabeth Cady Stanton – 1815-1902. Abolitionist and women's rights activist who formed a formidable partnership with Susan B. Anthony on behalf of temperance, abolition of slavery, and women's suffrage.

Walter Hines Page – 1855-1918. Journalist, publisher, and Ambassador to Great Britain during WWI. He influenced Woodrow Wilson to enter the Great War alongside Britain.

Albert Beveridge – 1862-1927. Senator from Indiana and an ardent imperialist. He favored annexation of the Philippines and other Progressive views of Theodore Roosevelt that included thinking the white race superior.

Thomas B. Reed – 1839-1902. Powerful Speaker of the House of Representatives and an adamant opponent of the Spanish-American War and the annexation of the Philippines. When President McKinley asked Congress for a Declaration of War against Spain he resigned.

Charles Eliot Norton – 1827-1908. Scholar and person of letters. Professor of history at Harvard and considered an expert on the history of Western Civilization.

Jack London – 1876-1916. American short-story author and Progressive socialist. His difficult and stressful life left him with physical disabilities. He died at age forty of kidney failure. He was one of the earliest writers to make a good living with his stories.

John Lancaster Spalding – 1840-1916. Catholic Bishop who helped found Catholic University of America in Washington, DC. He was Bishop of the Peoria Diocese of Illinois and a leader in education circles there.

Charles Woodmason – 1720-1789. Anglican missionary to the backwaters of South Carolina in the 1760's. He chronicled the primitive conditions of the early American colonists. They had no fit food; no clothes; no education to speak of. These colonists were fiercely independent.

Francis Wayland Parker – 1837-1902. Known as the father of Progressive education. A friend of John Dewey. He rejected rote learning, harsh discipline, and testing.

John Dewey – 1859-1952. Philosopher and founder of Progressive education. An atheist, he saw himself as a democratic socialist. One of the leading American thinkers of the 20th century with great impact on education theory and practice.

Mary Antin – 1881-1949. Jewish Russian immigrant to America at age thirteen who wrote and lectured on the experience of assimilation. Attended Columbia University and Barnard College.

Aaron Copland – 1900-1990. American composer considered to have brought American music into its own sphere. His music has become synonymous with the American experience. Considered by many to be the most influential American composer.

Sinclair Lewis – 1885-1951. American novelist and first American to win the Nobel Prize in Literature. A critic of American capitalism.

Mother Jones – 1837-1930. Mary Harris Jones. Irish labor movement organizer and social activist.

Helen Hunt Jackson – 1830-1885. Writer and social activist on behalf of the treatment of native-Americans by the national government of the United States.

W. E. B. Dubois – 1868-1963. Civil rights activist; helped found the NAACP; a Pan-Africanist, he fought the effects of European colonialism.

Marcus Garvey– 1887-1940. Black separatist from Jamaica who called for political unification of all Africans and a return of blacks to Africa. He opposed integration of the races.

Will Rogers – 1879-1935. American humorist and social commentator. A Cherokee from Oklahoma he was the highest paid movie star of his time.

Upton Sinclair – 1878-1968. American writer and Progressive socialist. He exposed unsanitary conditions in the meatpacking industry that led to the passage of the Pure Food and Drug Act and the Meat Inspection Act.

Jane Addams – 1860-1935. Wealthy Progressive social reformer and peace activist. Founded Hull House, a settlement house in Chicago that provided educational and cultural assistance to immigrant families. John Dewey was a close friend.

Marian Anderson – 1897-1993. Celebrated American contralto. Denied, in 1939, the use of Constitution Hall in Washington, DC because of race, she sang at the Lincoln Memorial to an audience of almost 100,000. Quintessential American citizen with great dignity and humility.

Henry David Thoreau – 1817-1862. American philosopher and leading Transcendentalist (to go beyond the boundary of experience). A disciple of Ralph Waldo Emerson. He believed in following what he considered "good" laws and disobeying "bad" laws.

Part II

ANNUIT COEPTIS

God favors our undertakings

7

The Godly

A dangerous ocean journey to the New World.

"We are entered into covenant with Him... We have taken out a commission... For this end, we must knit together ... We must hold each other in brotherly affection; we must be willing to rid ourselves of our excesses ... so that men shall say ... 'The Lord make it like that of New England.' For we must consider that we shall be like a City upon a Hill; the eyes of all people are on us. "[xxxiii]

JOHN WINTHROP (1588-1649) A MODELL OF CHRISTIAN CHARITY--1630

Can you imagine being in an advanced stage of pregnancy on a structurally questionable wooden vessel crowded with one-hundred and two passengers and two dogs living in the 'tween decks of the ship? Can you imagine giving birth at sea without privacy, in great agony, with foul food and water and with impudent crew members looking on? Elizabeth Hopkins did just that, and she arrived with her newborn at Cape Cod after a harrowing late fall voyage across the Atlantic, on November 11, 1620.[xxxiv]

It had already begun to snow in New England; no one had prepared for this type of cold. Instead of warm clothes they brought a few precious possessions from their home in Leiden, Holland – some chests, some chairs, some remembrances in lieu of the loved ones they had left behind. They came not as explorers or adventurers, as was true in Jamestown, but as families, ready to begin an important new "pure and simple" Christian life.

How do you say goodbye knowing that there will be no return; no re-uniting; no mercy on the sea; no surety of landing; and no knowledge of what, in practical terms, lay ahead? It would become a familiar state of being for countless colonists from England, Ireland, Scotland, Wales, Germany, and Holland. Later, it would be a familiar state of being for countless souls from West Africa to America and into the abyss of slavery.

What could be so important that one would voluntarily risk almost certain death for themselves and their children to make such a voyage? They knew the odds. At Jamestown thirteen years earlier seventy percent of the colonists died right away. During the starving time ninety-five percent of the colonists died gruesome deaths and cannibalism was not unknown. In fact, at the time of the Mayflower, of the three thousand or so colonists in Jamestown only six hundred had survived.[xxxv]

The answer is that the Separatists (or Pilgrims) loved God in a certain way and God led them to America. God was completely personal to these Separatists from the Anglican Church in England and its sterile Book of Common Prayer. They wanted to worship as they pleased. King James had practically thrown them out of the country as dangerous and they had gone to Holland to escape persecution. They lived in a type of commonwealth, and worked in the textile industry, for the most part, until black lung disease and overcrowded conditions began to move them toward leaving. They never wanted to be Dutch.

More importantly, they wanted to be on the winning side of the battle of Good against Evil. The Saints would prevail! The wickedness and depravity of humankind would bow to the powerful God of the chosen. To be on the right side of God – there could be no greater joy. It was not about this life but the next. Young children were left behind with relatives and friends. A more resilient, a more patient, a more persistent, a more dedicated group of English men and women, originally from Nottinghamshire, and exiled to Holland, can hardly be found.

Their charismatic leader who stayed behind was John Robinson. He wrote to them:

> *"So does the Lord call us in a singular manner upon occasions of such difficulty and danger as lie up you, to a both more narrow search and careful reformation of our ways in His sight, lest He, calling to remembrance our sins forgotten by us or unrepented of, take advantage against us and in judgment leave us for the same to*

be swallowed up in one danger or other; whereas on the contrary,
sin being taken away by earnest repentance and the pardon thereof
from the Lord, sealed up into a man's conscience by his spirit, great
shall be his security and peace in all dangers, sweet his comforts in
all distresses, with happy deliverance from all evil, whether in life
or in death."[xxxvi]

Either they lived to serve God, or they died to serve God. In any case God favored their undertaking and they hoped He was pleased. Didn't God lead the Israelites out of Egypt? Finally anchoring in Provincetown, they had lost few lives on the ship, due in part to the hygienic leadership of William Bradford. One death after they had anchored and were searching for a settlement sight was Dorothy Bradford, William's beloved wife, who, depressed and disconsolate at leaving behind their three-year old son John, went overboard and drowned in the sea. It is not known whether this was an accident or a suicide, but every event to the Pilgrims was either a statement or a sign from God.[xxxvii]

They had made it but there began to be serious problems. First, before they could even explore their surroundings, crew members and some passengers who were not Separatists began to question the authority of the whole voyage. They had a patent from the Virginia Company to land in Northern Virginia, not New England, so no real authority existed for their early colonizing efforts and many of them wanted to go home since they had missed their target and were getting increasingly sick. The Separatists felt otherwise and quickly created a document that could substitute as an authority that they all agreed to obey. This document was the Mayflower Compact.

"In the name of God, Amen. We whose names are underwritten, the
loyal subjects of our dread sovereign lord King James, by the grace
of God, of Great Britain, France, and Ireland, King, Defender of the
Faith, etc. Having undertaken for the glory of God, and
advancement of the Christian faith and honor of our king and
country, a voyage to plant the first colony in the northern part of
Virginia, do by these present, solemnly and mutually, in the
presence of God and one of another, covenant and combine

ourselves together into a civil body politic, for our better ordering and preservation and furtherance of the ends aforesaid: and by virtue hereof to enact, constitute, and frame such just and equal laws, ordinances, acts, constitutions, offices from time to time as shall be thought most meet and convenient for the general good of the colony; unto which we promise all due submission and obedience. In witness whereof we have hereunder subscribed our names, Cape Cod, 11th of November, in the year of the reign of our sovereign lord, King James, of England, France, and Ireland 18, and of Scotland 54. Anno Domini 1620."

Let us look at this compact more closely and perhaps in a different way. First and foremost, the Separatists were no fans of King James who had persecuted them mercilessly in England and sent them packing to Holland. They carried with them the Geneva Bible that King James ultimately had revised. All of this "loyal subjects" language really means that they were English, liked being English, and expected the King to honor the rights of their British citizenship. The language was also required to get the signatures of crew and non-Separatist passengers. Second, even with God spelled out at least four times, this is basically a secular document.

Compare the wording in the Mayflower Compact with the wording in the United States Constitution of 1787:

We do covenant and combine ourselves into a civil body politick.
   We do ordain and establish this Constitution.

For our better ordering and preservation
   To insure domestic tranquility, Provide for the common defense.

To enact such just and equal laws
   To establish justice

For the general good of the colonie
   To promote the general welfare

Unto which we promise all due submission and obedience

> *Senators and Representatives and members of the several State legislatures and all executive and judicial officers, both of the United States and of the several States, shall be bound to support this Constitution.*

What was undertaken for the "glorie of God and advancemente of the Christian faith" became a secular contract for governance by the consent of the governed. For those who signed the Mayflower Compact no religious questions were asked; what was asked was due obedience and submission to the laws of the colony and its leadership.

> *In witness whereof hereunder subscribed our names.*

The United States Constitution, however, incorporates a specific restriction against a religious test.

> *No religious Test shall ever be required as a Qualification to any Office or public Trust under the United States.*

Abraham Lincoln thought that the *Apple of Gold* was the Declaration of Independence framed in silver by the United States Constitution. But if we really look at it perhaps the *Apple of Gold* is really the Mayflower Compact and the United States Constitution as bookends of secular theory regarding a new governing order for the ages. What are some of the main component parts of this new Order?

1. The word of the individual, by oath or affirmation, not religious affiliation, matters. Personal virtue is the indispensable glue that binds us into a civil body politic for our preservation and good order. We as citizens submit personally by our word of honor to secular authority for the good of the whole.
2. Government by the un-coerced consent of the governed; this implies consent can be withdrawn if government does not serve the greater good in the opinion of the governed.
3. A written agreement between the government and its citizens through the signatures of citizen representatives.

Enlightenment notions of statecraft common to the 16th, 17th, and 18th centuries, having emerged from under the heavy cloud of religious governance, percolated to the surface at our earliest moments of colonization and birth as a nation. A person's religious or ethical views go to the personal honor required to submit and obey to what is secularly commanded, if what is commanded is moral and ethical. The restraint on secular government is not only the structures created for "just" (impartial) process but the overriding natural and moral law which undergirds secular governance in the first place. What an interesting overlapping and interconnected concept!

It hadn't been tried before, in part, because there were strong notions about the capacity of human beings, given their nature, to exercise the discipline, restraint, good judgment, and obedience to the Rule of Law necessary for it to work. Better to rule with an iron religious fist and take personal options out of it.

The Separatist adventure in 1620 was lucky enough to be led by a particularly talented group of good, dedicated, educated, and honorable men that, by happenstance, appear at the same time with the same commitment. This bookend of our republican notions, the Mayflower Compact, is not as honored as the Constitution in 1787, but it is no less important even though the utopian community the Pilgrims hoped to establish in America failed. Human behavior and utopian dreams are always in conflict.

The Godly

William Bradford tells the story of this earliest experiment from its hopeful but tragic beginnings to its inevitable end. What began as communal gave way to individual, and no amount of incentives offered could keep the community together in its attempts to re-create the simple Christian life.

> *"In these hard and difficult beginnings they found some discontents and murmurings arise among some, and mutinous speeches and carriages in other; but they were soon quelled and overcome by the wisdom, patience, and just and equal carriage of things by the governor and better part which clave faithfully together in the main.*
>
> *But that which was sad and lamentable was that in two or three months' time half of their company died being infected with the scurvy and other diseases ... there were but six or seven sound persons who to their commendations ... spared no pains night or day... made them fires, dressed them meat, made their beds, washed their loathsome clothes, clothed and unclothed them. In a word, did all the homely and necessary offices for them which dainty and queasy stomachs cannot endure to hear named; and all this willingly and cheerfully, without any grudging in the least, showing herein their true love unto their friends and brethren; a rare example and worthy to be remembered.*
>
> *But about the 16th of March, a certain Indian came boldly among them. His name was Samoset. He told them also of another Indian whose name was Squanto ..and made way for the coming of their great sachem, called Massasoit, who came with the aforesaid Squanto; they made a peace with him (which has now continued this twenty-four years) in these terms:*
>
> 1. *That neither he nor any of his should injure or do hurt to any of their people*
> 2. *That if any of his did hurt to any of theirs, he should send the offender that they might punish him*
> 3. *That if anything were taken away from any of theirs; he should cause it to be restored ...*
> 4. *If any did unjustly war against him, they would aid him.*

5. *He should send to his neighbors, confederates to certify them of this, that they might be likewise comprised in the conditions of peace*
6. *That when their men came to them, they should leave their bows and arrows behind.*

   Squanto continued with them and was their interpreter and was a special instrument sent of God for their good beyond their expectation ... He directed them how to set their corn, where to take fish, and to procure other commodities, and was also their pilot to bring them to unknown places for their profit, and never left them till he died." xxxviii

WILLIAM BRADFORD, 1620-1647

OF PLYMOUTH PLANTATION

Squanto was a great and just man who arrived at exactly the right time for the survival of the first utopian experiment in English America. There would be many more such attempts in the future. There is no question that the native peoples along the Atlantic seaboard and specifically around Cape Cod could have destroyed the entire Separatist adventure. If you can imagine agonizing hunger and cold; if you can imagine uncontrolled intestinal distress without relief; if you can imagine never being clean; if you can imagine deep darkness and throbbing fear; if you can imagine trying to find the strength to bury the dead and protect the precious chest of drawers instead of warm clothes that you brought from Holland; if you can imagine the heartbreak of knowing that the English pea seeds you hoped would sprout were not going to work in Massachusetts soil; if you can imagine being at wit's end and close to death then you have a feel for this handful of people wanting to be worthy of God in a foreign land with their only hope a devout faith and savvy leadership.

The roles of Massasoit, a very powerful sachem, and Squanto, the loving teacher of survival, cannot be exaggerated. Massasoit was very aware that with one word the whole party would be killed instantly, regardless of the European weapons and skill of the military leader of the Separatists, Miles Standish. What made Massasoit decide to let them live? By the time the native peoples decided that they had had enough of the Europeans, (even with their interesting pots and tools and guns) and planned a multi-tribe conspiracy to attack and annihilate them, it was too late. The conspiracy was crushed.

In truth, the Separatists and the Pokanokets lived in peace until Massasoit's death. Their agreement was not broken. Their words of honor held. At one point, when it was thought that the great leader would die and unsettle the whole arrangement, Edward Winslow hiked to the sachem's village through the snow, to assist in trying to save him. Facing certain death if Massasoit died, Winslow slowly brought him back to health by feeding him a concocted broth that cleaned out his whole system. It worked. He lived. The Europeans were thought to have great healing powers and held the respect of native-Americans necessary to achieve survival for another day.[xxxix]

Even with this help, the Plymouth Colony did not survive. It ultimately dispersed into the larger, more powerful, better funded Massachusetts Bay Colony. William Bradford lived long enough to see the inevitable and wrote painfully about it. They had survived epidemics with no medicine; they had survived severe droughts that threatened their entire food supply; they had re-built large storage structures after massive fires; but they could not survive the development of individual farms and the loss of the communal that had been their original design and strength.

Bradford writes that persons of questionable quality arrived at their shores and used precious resources that had been painstakingly preserved. Several so-called religious leaders came with what were to them heretical religious views. Several left the colony and created a new one, Wessagusset, twenty miles away only to have to be rescued from their personal sexual depravities and starving bodies at great cost to the colony.

There began to be signs of human behaviors unacceptable to the Godly. The discipline began to crack as colonists moved farther and farther apart and lost touch with the church and its practices. Some did not pray as required; some did not attend church as required; some did not participate in the Days of Humiliation as required; some lost their morals and their sense of tight closeness to the group.

One of the miracles of the Separatist experiment is that it was relatively peaceful. The predictable culture clash between Europe and native-Americans was handled by honorable people and strict discipline including official land sales to the colonists through an official Council. The rest of the Atlantic coast was not so lucky. Colonist versus native-American wars waged brutally from Virginia to New York. Both sides participated in bloody attacks and massacres – the Pequot War; Kieft's War; King Philip's War; and on and on. In Jamestown, Virginia, settled in 1607, although a different group of colonists altogether from the Plymouth settlement, relative peace existed with the powerful Powhatan and regular intercourse between settlers and native-Americans existed. When Powhatan's brother, Opechancanough, took over, he began to plan for an all-out assault on the coastal settlements to re-assert authority and confine the English settlement to a small area that could be controlled.[xl]

In 1622 he attacked, and normally friendly and known native-Americans picked up any weapon they could find and killed everyone they could on the spot. Settlers were defaced and hacked into pieces and otherwise so brutally murdered that the shock lingered for a very long time and revenge smoldered. About three-hundred fifty colonists died horrible deaths. Any Christian view of benevolence toward native-Americans was obliterated and the memory of the attack lingered for decades.[xli]

Similarly, but farther north, skirmishes between native-Americans and spread-out settlers finally led to a revenge raid described by Captain John Underhill regarding the Pequot War, 1636:

"Drawing neere to the Fort yielded up ourselves to God, and intreated his assistance in so waightie and enterprize. We set on our march to surround the Fort... giving a volley of shotte...at breake of day...[that] bred in them such a terrour, that they brake forth into a most dolefull cry... every man being bereaved of pitty fell upon the worke without compassion considering the bloud they had shed of our native Country-men about thirty persons downe fell men, women, and children, those that scaped us, fell into the hands of the Indians, that were in the reere of us it is repourted there were about

The Godly

foure hundred soules in this Fort, and not about five of them escaped out of our hands."[xlii]

The City upon a Hill; the undertaking watched by Him; brotherly affection toward all encouraged; excess toward all discouraged; but in the end, human action, reaction, justification, revenge, all played out in maximum amounts of blood and burning flesh by those that came to settle and by those who were already here.

8

Religion, Morality, and the United States Constitution

The conflict between establishment and free exercise of religion.

"It is better that the Commonwealth be fashioned to the setting forth of God's house, which is His church, than to accommodate the Church frame to the civil state. Democracy, I do not conceive, that ever God did ordain as fit government either for church or commonwealth. If the people be governors, who shall be governed? [He] setteth up theocracy ... as the best form of government in the commonwealth as well as in the church."[xliii]

JOHN COTTON, (1585-1652) 1636, IN A LETTER TO BRITISH LORD SAYE

Of the intellectual frictions, one or the other of which prevails, the role of organized religious structures relative to the American system is one of the most interesting and the least understood.

John Cotton felt strongly that while England was governed by "gentlemen" with the capacity, heritage, and personal resources to rule on behalf of the people; in America, that role should fall to "men of faithful integrity to God and the state to preserve the same." This is the nuance that was a bit different than practices in Europe.

Integrity to God in America meant integrity to Protestantism, mostly, not a sect of Protestantism. What happened in colonial America, except Rhode Island, is what felt like second-class citizenship if you were not practicing that form of Protestantism in that locality. As reflected in the First Amendment to the United States Constitution there would be no national state religion. There would be no Lutheran or

Anglican or Roman Catholic or Presbyterian America as in Sweden, England, Spain or Scotland.

Establishment of religion in America came to mean financial support for religion generally, not a legal selection of a sect (though there were specific tax-supported sects in some states until the mid-19th century), John Cotton's wish notwithstanding. The exodus of Protestants from Europe, intent on separating or purifying the Church of England, could be considered part of a Utopian movement whose desire for un-conflicted supportive relationships and simple worship compelled them to start afresh in the New World. William Bradford and others tried hard to keep their little family of believers communal, sharing, caring, and Godly.

The Pilgrims and Puritans were an entirely different group of colonists than the second and third sons of aristocrats or other types that came to Jamestown and elsewhere. Yet religious or not, all the early colonies needed "quality" people to tend, prune, and develop the tender shoots of their existence. Survival itself was initially the only thing that mattered. Various ships arrived at fledgling doorsteps full of survivors of passage but with nothing else. Their rations gone, their clothes but rags, they had to be tended to and incorporated into the whole whether costly to that whole or not. Some ships brought ravaging infectious diseases that added further injury to an already delicate existence and sent those diseases into the native populations.

Whether as solemn Calvinists or eager adventurers, there is in Americans the ever-present "begin the world anew" (more specifically, begin *my* world anew) aspect to our character. There is also a strong religious component in our history rooted deeply in failed experiments and in edgy non-conformists like Roger Williams, who stirred up early colonial communities in Boston, Salem, and Plymouth with his "dangerous" notions of religious tolerance, all the while seeking his version of "true religion."

Although ultimately crafting the same power centers that they had left in the "old" world, many early religious communities contained a core of the truly pious, the sweetly sincere, and the very decent that represent qualities that human beings are capable of. Early on they were led and protected by competent and talented men and women, many of whom were excellently educated and highly intelligent. This combination of sincerity and goodness along with skilled leadership and just plain luck got them through the most critical of times.

William Bradford would say, of course, that it was not luck but Divine guidance under a predestined plan carried out properly that worked its magic in the Plymouth Plantation founding. The seeds were sown early, however, for toleration, if not full acceptance, for any number of non-Catholic versions of Christianity and their emphasis on a personal relationship with God through Scripture. The experience also emphasizes that leadership in some of the earliest of settlements was mostly by "believers" not by nobility.

These concepts are reflected in our national Constitution of 1787:

Article I, Section 9

No Title of Nobility shall be granted by the United States:

Article I, Section 10

No state ... shall grant any Title of Nobility

Article VI

No religious test shall ever be required as a Qualification to any Office or public Trust under the United States

John Cotton believed that governance that was once thought of as the purview of the aristocracy, whose families carried through with these responsibilities for generations, or for a monarchy, is now the purview of the Godly of any class of person. His view was that without persons who are faithful to God – not necessarily to a church – the State would ultimately suffer because the State represents power and power corrupts the person. A belief and obedience to God, then, might check that corruption for the common good. Hence our national motto: In God We Trust.[xliv]

To some modern American minds, separation of church and state may imply a separation of the person from a connection to God, not separation of ecclesiastical law from positive law or government supported religion. What it really means in the American system is a complete liberty of conscience (including the liberty not to believe) and free exercise of religious practice not in conflict with positive law.

This *irony* of what, from our earliest beginnings as a nation, many believed to be indispensable to peace and good order but whose loss we nevertheless tolerate as a fundamental liberty, makes some of the views of Roger Williams and some of the views of John Cotton interestingly compatible. Both thought a belief in God necessary and fundamental to law; Roger Williams expanded that concept to include tolerance of how that belief is made manifest in a religious organization.

Before security and order were fully achieved in the Massachusetts Bay Colony, the following school law was ordered by its leaders:

> *"It being one chief project of the old deluder, Satan, to keep men from the knowledge of the scriptures it is therefore ordered that every township in this jurisdiction that the Lord has increased to fifty households shall appoint one within their town to teach all such children whose wages shall be paid by parents or masters of such children. "*[xlv]

This law passed in 1647 although the first school laws were passed in the colony in 1642. And in the same era the Massachusetts General Court, 1641, passed the *Liberties of the Massachusetts Collonie in New England,* one of the provisions being a nod to some religious tolerance:

> *"All the people of god within this Jurisdiction who are not in a church way, and be orthodox in Judgement, and not scandalous in life, shall have full libertie to gather themselves into a church estaite. Provided they do it in a Christian way, with due observation of the rules of Christ revealed in his word."*[xlvi]

In New Amsterdam, 1657, while under the leadership of Peter Stuyvesant and the Dutch, Quakers from Flushing, New York were barred from practicing their faith. Some citizens in sympathy with them wrote a letter to colonial authorities.

> *"You have been pleased to send up to us a command that we should not receive any of those people called Quakers, because they are ... seducers of the people. The law of love, peace, and liberty in the states extending to Jews, Turks, and Egyptians, as they are considered the sons of Adam, which is the outward state of Holland; so our desire is not to offend one of His little ones in whatsoever form, whether Presbyterian, Independent, Baptist or Quaker; but shall be glad to see anything of God in any of them, desiring to do unto all men as we desire all men should do unto us, which is the true law both of church and state."[xlvii]*

Over one hundred years later in 1785, James Madison wrote a "Remonstrance Against Religious Assessments" as a prelude to the anticipated "Virginia Statute for Religious Freedom" authored by Thomas Jefferson. Madison's argument is that Christianity cannot be coerced through political means based on the Law of Natural Rights.

> *"The Religion, then, of every man must be left to the conviction and conscience of every man; and it is the right of every man to exercise it as these may dictate. This right is in its nature an unalienable right. It is the duty of every man to render to the Creator such homage and such only as he believes to be acceptable to him.* "[xlviii]

Said another way by Jefferson and enacted by the Virginia General Assembly, 1786:

> *"We the General Assembly of Virginia do enact, that no man shall be compelled to frequent or support any religious worship, place, or ministry whatsoever, nor shall be enforced, restrained, molested, or burdened in his body or goods, nor shall otherwise suffer, on account of his religious opinions or belief; but that all men shall be free to profess, and by argument to maintain, their opinions in matters of religion, and that the same shall in no wise diminish, enlarge, or affect their civil capacities."[xlix]*

Evidently "support" did not include financial as Virginia supported the Anglican Church in that state through taxation. Jefferson's overall view, however, is what we established and ordained in the United States Constitution of 1787 with the Amendments of 1791, was applicable to the federal government but not the states.[1]

Amendment I

Congress shall make no law respecting an establishment of religion or prohibiting the free exercise thereof.

So, here is one of the persistent conflicts in the American experience. If John Cotton is correct and there is joy when the righteous are in authority and calamity when they are not, how does society assure itself of one and discourage the other?

It was stated in the 1787 passage of the Northwest Ordinance, that "religion, morality, and knowledge being necessary to good government and the happiness of mankind, schools and the means of education shall forever be encouraged." Religion and morality, it was implied, are indispensable to good government and not separate. Madison and Jefferson are saying something entirely different and separating them distinctly. James Madison in his remonstrance to the general assembly stated:

"We maintain therefore that in matters of Religion, no man's right is abridged by the institution of Civil Society and that Religion is wholly exempt from its cognizance."[li]

What we are asked to consider are: First, do those public servants who are religious serve society with mostly more integrity than those who are not? If "no" or "not sure," from what other source might integrity be obtained by a public servant? Second, are the schools mentioned in the Northwest Ordinance connected to religion, morality, and knowledge or just to knowledge and morality?

The "righteous in authority" is another way of saying that the American system requires virtue in her public servants and virtue in her sovereign citizens. This view is universal among the Founders and others that support the American experiment in representative constitutional democracy.

> *"If men were angels, no government would be necessary. If angels were to govern men, neither external nor internal controls on government would be necessary. In framing government, which is to be administered by men over men, the great difficulty lies in this: You must first enable the government to control the governed; and in the next place, oblige it to control itself."*[lii]
>
> JAMES MADISON, FEDERALIST PAPER #51

It is unnecessary for us to answer the elementary question about the nature of humanity in full. Philosophers have different answers as to whether human beings are innately evil due to "original sin" but can learn goodness; whether human beings are neutral (blank slates) and form character with circumstance; or whether human beings are in the image of God but become corrupt with a corrupt world or some combination of all of these theories.

What we do know is that the Founders thought human beings had a depravity that could be checked by reason through the strictures of positive law and that morality in the citizenry was important, actually most thought religion was important, but most also thought that religious views should nevertheless not be in the purview of government at all as an element of personal liberty.

This view begs the question, then how do we create the moral citizenry necessary for representative democracy to work without religion guiding those citizens to that morality?

The answer lies in the other component to the moral training of our society that came to us through Aristotle, (384-322 BCE) and other Greek philosophers. Aristotle's view was known and understood by the Founders and plays an important role in the philosophical foundations of our system. Aristotle felt that there are universal ethics, (the opposite of situational ethics), that human beings seek happiness, and that happiness for human beings lies in living a virtuous life. It so happens that a virtuous life also supports and complements a governmental system that values liberty.

In Aristotle's view, citizens can be taught virtue through habits that lead to moral will and are translated into personal conduct. He encouraged them to find the golden mean -- behavior that lies between extremes. *Courage* lies between the extremes of cowardice and recklessness; *temperance* lies between deprivation and insensibility; *justice* lies between one's rights being trampled on and trampling on other's rights; *friendship* lies between fawning and arguing.

Virtue to Aristotle meant doing the right thing in the right way to the right person in the right degree. Aristotle thought that human beings are social animals and that virtue is critical to good citizenship. So here is our alternative to religion guiding our citizenry to morality. Society can teach the virtues to its children based, not on a fear of or love for a higher power, but on the proper purposes to which human beings naturally aspire. Later virtues were added by Christianity (*faith*, *hope*, and *charity*) and still later by Jane Austen (*amiability*) and Benjamin Franklin (*industry*). Aristotle did not think faith and reason incompatible and the major religions of Judaism and Islam encompass some of the same thinking.

William Bradford was particularly interested in an early Jewish philosopher, Moses ben Maimon, 1135-1204, and the whole story of Hebrew experience. He saw it as compatible with leading his flock to a new untainted land and some of his preserved writings are his own Hebrew translations.

The approach to this quandary in our Federal Constitution of 1787, at a time when allegiance to a religion or Christian sect dominated one's personal life, was handled by the very structure of our system known as Federalism. This structure divides power between the national government and state governments. Meant to diffuse power as a check on its concentration, especially concentration of power at the national level, the Bill of Rights, which includes the prohibition against establishing religion, affected only the national government, not state governments. State governments were free to establish tax support for Christian sects or tax support for one sect and the 1st Amendment was no bar to this common practice. Madison attempted to extend this ban to the states but was voted down at the Constitutional Convention.

By custom, then, although Aristotle's virtues could have been taught, since schools were in the province of state power and the 1st Amendment Establishment Clause did not apply, public education regularly and almost universally attempted to create a moral citizenry through prayer, through teaching scripture, through religious music, and the celebration of religious holidays. Parents were very comfortable with the notion that what was taught at home was being reinforced at public schools (*in loco parentis*). This practice, mostly in reciting the Lord's Prayer, continued for over three hundred years until a dramatic and revolutionary doctrine, in much of the public's mind, gained preeminence in the Supreme Court.

It is known as the Incorporation Doctrine and it was applied to a case in 1962 that ended the centuries-old habit of praying in public schools. Later it was applied to prayer before football games, baccalaureate exercises, and Christmas displays, pageants, and parades, and a host of other things, including a prayer at the beginning of the school day along with the Pledge of Allegiance.[liii]

The Incorporation Doctrine is a product of interpretation of the Constitution, not of the text of the Constitution itself. It means that the Bill of Rights, or the first ten Amendments to the United States Constitution, meant to apply only to the actions of a federal government actor, apply, in part, to state government actors by being "incorporated" into the Due Process Clause of the 14th Amendment as applicable to the states.

This was Madison's original intention finally made manifest by a rather awkward and mysterious view of the emanations and penumbras of textual rights that ought to be civil protections against state governments. Which ones of the rights fell into this imaginary funnel has been up to separate Supreme Courts. The Incorporation Doctrine represents one of the *mysteries* that we must become comfortable with in understanding the United States Constitution. It is best understood to add teeth to the post-Civil War Amendments that granted citizenship rights to freed slaves.

Amendment XIV, Section 1
No State shall make or enforce any law which shall abridge
the privileges or immunities of citizens of the United States; nor
shall any State deprive any person of life, liberty, or property,
without due process of law.

"Liberty" in the 14th Amendment included, according to various Supreme Courts, some of the rights in the Bill of Rights, including the prohibition on "establishing" religion by either the federal or any state government or state government actors such as public schools.

The reason the Founders limited application of the Bill of Rights to the federal government is that the West tended to organize society around a Church and a King. So, the Founders, by dividing the atom of power between the national and state and local governments, could have it both ways. We would not have a King or Queen at all nor would we have an official Church on the federal level but on the state level establishing religion was allowed but left to each state. Prayer in school was universal in states as one method of teaching moral duty to students who would later become the moral citizens the Republic needed. The Incorporation Doctrine ended that concept.

We are a long way now from John Cotton; we are a long way now from William Bradford; we are even a long way from Roger Williams. If it is true that a moral citizenry is necessary for our system to properly function, we have yet to decide comfortably how to go about publicly educating for it and whether religion or something else is the basis for it.

Alexis de Tocqueville, 1831, made these observations regarding religion and politics in America on a visit he made to the United States to study our penal system.

> *"One would think that men who had sacrificed their friends, their*
> *family, and their native land to a religious conviction would be*
> *wholly absorbed in the pursuit of the treasure which they had just*
> *purchased at so high a price. And yet we find them seeking with*
> *nearly equal zeal for material wealth and moral good – for well-*
> *being and freedom on earth, and salvation in heaven... Religion*
> *perceives that civil liberty affords a noble exercise to the faculties*

of man, and that the political world is a field prepared by the Creator for the efforts of mind...Religion never more surely establishes its empire than when it reigns in the hearts of men unsupported by aught beside its native strength...Liberty regards religion as its companion in all its battles and its triumphs – as the cradle of its infancy, and the divine source of its claims. It considers religion as the safeguard of morality, and morality as the best security of law, and the surest pledge of the duration of freedom."[liv]

It might be debated today whether religion is necessary to teach morality. To the early Pilgrims and Puritans, it was basic and essential and virtually the same thing. Many colonists left comfortable homes in Europe to experience a religious "new beginning" in collaboration with fellow believers. Many others came as adults to escape something or to find economic wealth, and many children came alone, as orphans, to try and make their way in a wild and scary New World.

9

An Expanding America in Conflict with Itself

We venture into the waters of imperialism.

"I say that when you against their will say that freedom as we conceive it, not freedom as they conceive it, public interest as we conceive it, not as they conceive it, shall prevail, and that if it does not we are to force it on them at the cannon's mouth – I say that nation which undertakes that plea and says it is subduing these men for their own good when they do not want to be subdued for their good will encounter the awful and terrible rebuke, 'Beware of the leaven of the Pharisee', which is hypocrisy."[lv]

SENATOR GEORGE HOAR (1826-1904), 1899

By the end of the 18th century, coinciding with the death of George Washington, the American Revolution (against monarchy) and the American Constitution (ratified with citizen consent) was the gold standard of Enlightenment thinking and a beacon that lit the way for other revolutions in South America and Europe.

Our story as a new nation during the following century is all energy, all growth, all innovation, all consolidation, broken in half by the final purge of slavery and the reconstruction of the slave states that followed. Reconstruction itself was a very difficult and uneven time. Many in the North craved a merciless revenge. Federalism as a concept became tilted toward federal power and has remained so. Export crops were not destroyed; wage labor supplanted slavery but felt, often, like the same thing.

The United States Constitution was amended to bring full citizenship and voting rights to former slaves, though these rights were not fully realized for another one hundred plus years. There is not *de jure* (by law) racial discrimination in the United States today though racial reconciliation remains an ongoing challenge for people of good will from both races.

Each element of the 19th century in America and in Europe is worthy of intense scholarship. War with native-Americans continued throughout. Like an overloaded small boat, the attitude toward native-Americans rocked back and forth as weight shifted between friend, enemy, inconvenience, ward, finally reaching shore in the 20th century with citizenship (1924), preservation of tribal integrity (1934), and an end to domestic dependent ward status (1953). The westward expansion of the nation was brutal and unrelenting; always with a nod toward Christian benevolence as well as toward assimilation and education, but in reality, a confiscation (including legitimate purchase) of land from very distinct and differing indigenous peoples.

Former European holdings in North America were brought into the nation over time. Texas became an independent republic (1836) and then a state in the Union (1845) after much antagonism with Mexico. What may appear as a giant land grab for the American Southwest and the Oregon Territory was in reality a very careful dance around the issue of admission of slave and free states and the balance of power between the North and the South that that distinction represented. The Mexican American War was a short, brutal, cession of land for about 15 million dollars and the assumption of claims from Americans against Mexico. Catholic Spain gave up her hold on the continental United States. France had done so with the Louisiana Purchase (1803).

New notions emerged in the West regarding political rights for women (Wyoming, 1869, voting rights). The women's movement had begun.

"Man [male] is in such a labyrinth of contradictions ... he is so befogged on the whole question of maidens, wives, and mothers that, from pure benevolence, we should relieve him from this troublesome branch of legislation ... But, you say, we would not have woman

exposed to the grossness and vulgarity of public life ... When you talk, gentlemen, of sheltering woman from the rough winds and revolting scenes of real life, you must be either talking for effect or wholly ignorant of what the facts of life are. The man ... is known to the woman... when alone in the darkness and solitude and gloom of night she has trembled on her own threshold awaiting the return of a husband from his midnight revels ... when stepping from her chamber she has beheld her royal monarch, her lord and master – her legal representative – the protector of her property, her home, her children, and her person, down on his hands and knees slowly crawling up the stairs. Behold him in her chamber – in her bed! The fairy tale of Beauty and the Beast is far too often realized in life. Gentlemen, such scenes as woman has witnessed at her own fireside where no eye save Omnipotence could pity, no strong arm could help, can never be realized at the polls, never equaled elsewhere this side of the bottomless pit."[lvi]

ELIZABETH CADY STANTON, 1860,

IN A SPEECH TO THE NEW YORK LEGISLATURE

The South lay prostrate while the North consolidated commercial power and wealth and for many decades had complete control of national policy as southern representation was very slowly brought back into Congress and its influence felt. The American black, an equal partner in creating the agrarian wealth foundational to American prosperity, began the long journey, with excellent leadership, of understanding how to traverse the cultural minefield that is America.[lvii]

The United States, after the War of 1812, was "relatively" peaceful for eight decades, and used this time to incubate, foster, massage, educate, and form what emerged by the end of the century – America as a potential world player. At this very pinnacle of achievement, the next great moral dilemma emerged. Would the United States embrace imperialism? Would the United States follow the example of the European powers that we disdained at our founding, to conquer, control, exploit, and suppress other sovereign nations because we had the strength to do so? Having just emerged, painfully, from our first great moral dilemma, slavery, would we jump headlong into the next?

Jump headlong we did – as if "that old deluder Satan" the Massachusetts Puritans were so worried about reached out an alluring hand and invited us to dance. How could a "good" people, with roots firmly secured in the fine earth of Scripture, pull itself up and out of that nutrient-rich and hydrated environment into the relentless dry winds of a moral desert?

The safeguards of our unwritten, moral, and Constitutional law could not and did not contain us. The American people willed a return to what they had once rejected as un-republican and un-American. I am speaking, of course, of the Spanish-American War and its aftermath.

Walter Hines Page, Editor of the *Atlantic Monthly* in an 1898 editorial wrote.

> *"The continued progress of the race in the equalization of opportunity and in well-being depends on democratic institutions, of which we, under God, are yet, in spite of all our shortcomings, the chief beneficiaries and custodians. Our greatest victory will not be over Spain but over ourselves – to show once more that even in its righteous wrath the republic has the virtue of self-restraint ... At every great emergency in our history we have had men equal to the duties that faced us. The men of the Revolution were the giants of their generation. Our Civil War brought forward the most striking personality of the century. As during a period of peace, we did not forget our courage and efficiency in war, so we believe, during a period of routine domestic politics we have not lost our capacity for the largest statesmanship. The great merit of democracy is that out of its multitudes, who have all had a chance for natural development, there arise, when occasion demands, stronger and wiser men that any class-governed societies have ever bred."*[lviii]

What emerged was Theodore Roosevelt, Jr., born in 1858 to the famously wealthy Roosevelt family that first arrived in Dutch New York in 1649. Teddy was physically fragile and was home-schooled until entering Harvard. He was spoiled; he was rich; he was snobbish; he was dandified; he was intelligent; and he was ambitious.

He married the beautiful Alice Lee at the age of twenty-two; took a five-month long honeymoon cruise to Europe; and found time to work on one of his many books during that time, *The Naval War of 1812*. He went to Columbia law school briefly and there found the justification for himself that he so desperately needed. He embraced the notion that his race had a duty to conquer "inferior" peoples and to lead them into the benevolent womb of the Anglo-Saxon Protestant and there be groomed and guided toward some form of civilized advancement.[lix]

> "It is a noble land that God has given us ... It is a mighty people that He has planted on this soil; a people sprung from the most masterful blood of history; a people perpetually revitalized by the virile, man-producing working folk of all the earth; a people imperial by virtue of their power, by right of their institutions, by authority of their heaven-directed purposes -the propagandists and not the misers of liberty . . . Hawaii is ours; Puerto Rico is to be ours; at the prayer of the people, Cuba will finally be ours; in the islands of the East, even to the gates of Asia ... It is the tide of God's great purposes made manifest in the instincts of our race, whose present phase is our personal profit, but whose far-off end is the redemption of the world and the Christianization of mankind ... Fellow Americans, we are God's chosen people...We cannot retreat from any soil where Providence has unfurled our banner; it is ours to save that soil for liberty and civilization."[lx]

ALBERT BEVERIDGE,
IN AN 1898 SENATORIAL CAMPAIGN SPEECH.

Teddy Roosevelt believed in these ideas to the core. His father had convinced him that his virility as a man and the virility of the American male, in general, were at stake. American men had become soft. They had lost their ancient barbarian virtues. "Over-civilized" was the word. War was the answer. Teddy, Assistant Secretary of the Navy, pushed President McKinley mercilessly toward war with Spain, a weak European colonial power, engaged in a protracted war of independence with both Cuban and Filipino freedom fighters. America sent a ship into Havana harbor to try and force an end to the conflict. It blew up in February and by April the war was on. Only much later was it determined that Spain had not sunk the *Maine*, a fire in a coal bunker was the probable culprit. It did not really matter; many Americans wanted war to reinvigorate her "manhood."[lxi]

In 1898 President McKinley requested a declaration of war even though Spain had indicated it would bow to American demands and sue for peace.

> *"I ask Congress to authorize and empower the President to take measures to secure a full and final termination of hostilities between the government of Spain and the people of Cuba ... and to use the military and naval forces of the United States as may be necessary for these purposes."*[lxii]

Article I, Section 8

The Congress shall have Power to declare War

War with Spain did not last long. There emerged the first media-concocted public relations scheme in the form of the Rough Riders led by Leonard Wood with Teddy Roosevelt in the saddle as a brave American fighting for the righteous Cubans against colonial Spain. The Senate promised self-rule for the Cuban people in the form of the Teller Amendment but later changed its mind.

In the Philippines, Admiral Dewey steamed into Manilla Bay, made a deal with the Spanish to fake opposition and then went inland with troops to conquer the very people who thought we were their friends. We were not. We had become an imperial power and we wanted the Philippines as an avenue to Chinese trade. We killed, raped, and water-boarded one to three million Filipinos. We created a military protectorate under the leadership of Lieutenant General Arthur McArthur, Jr.[lxiii]

Finally, we turned the Philippines over to civilian control headed by William Howard Taft who became Governor, for the purpose of "helping" an inferior race of people become "able" to self-govern. They resisted our help and were cut down until they surrendered. William Howard Taft eventually became President of the United States and later Chief Justice of the Supreme Court. It was not until after World War II that the Philippines became an independent nation.[lxiv]

And so, America stepped over the line and outside the box of the founding generation's values and cautions and took its place as a world power, with all the intrigue, machinations, subtleties, entanglements, and unintended consequences that the decision to do so entailed. As with slavery, there were many important voices in opposition.

> *"But every rapid up-rise of empire was the sure precursor of a rapid fall ... you may see the United States of America as they looked while they were still but the colonies of another country and when they began their struggle for freedom. It is a very empty map ... We have added to that little strip shore ... we have been content to make what we could out of what we have go...all history is against the perpetuity of nations...there seems to be but one source of destruction, and that is the failure of each section of a great country to keep abreast of the others...and to promote always the common interest. . .That there are vast differences between the ideas and wants of our separate regions is not so well known...These differences are really differences in civilization...the great aim of a nation should be...to assimilate to a common standard. . .There is no need of hurry...Our strength grows with our years. . .those empires which hope for eternity can wait."[lxv]*

> THOMAS B. REED,
> SPEAKER OF THE HOUSE OF REPRESENTATIVES 1897,

> *"We believe that America has something better to offer to mankind than those aims she is now pursuing, and we mourn her desertion of ideals which were not selfish nor limited in their application, but which are of universal worth and validity. She has lost her unique position as a potential leader in the progress of civilization and has taken up her place simply as one of the grasping and selfish nations of the present day. We all know how far she has fallen short in the*

past of exhibiting in her conduct a fidelity to those ideals which she professed, but some of us, at least, had not lost the hope that she would ultimately succeed in becoming more faithful to them.[lxvi]

CHARLES ELIOT NORTON, HARVARD PROFESSOR, 1899

There were signs of the impending imperialism. Having closed the frontier with no more western lands to conquer, some opinion makers and others looked west, to our Manifest Destiny, to always go west until all civilization is within our orbit. The Pacific Ocean became our new highway to what was "rightfully" ours.

In 1875 a treaty was signed with Hawaii granting us rights to military bases. In 1893 the sugar barons saw to it that United States Marines dethroned Queen Liliuokalani and we annexed Hawaii in 1898. The justifying questions were asked and answered. Would it not be better that we take over rather than she goes to Japan or Germany? Had we not purchased Alaska from Russia in 1868? Does all territory owned by the United States have to be contiguous?[lxvii]

The Mexican War in 1845 established the Rio Grande as our border with Mexico and was considered by many, including General Grant, to be an immoral invasion of another country at great cost of life. On our own soil, there was the massacre at Wounded Knee in 1890. During the Indian Wars after the Civil War, William Tecumseh Sherman ordered everyone slaughtered including women, children, and the elderly. Many people thought these actions represented progress and survival of the fittest.

Step by step and once accomplished, the "old deluder" was able to convince our President that he did not have to take the process steps as outlined in the United States Constitution that created a check on the executive branch and are an important yellow light.

Article II, Section 2

The President shall have Power, by and with the Advice and Consent of the Senate, to make Treaties, provided two thirds of the Senators present concur.

President Roosevelt proceeded to conduct foreign policy outside of Congress and outside of the State Department and outside of any check provided for by our federal Constitution. He just took Panama from Columbia under the auspices of the Monroe Doctrine (South America is a sphere of influence of the United States). He supported Japan over Russia in the precursor to World War I and supported Japan's takeover of Korea. He supported a Monroe Doctrine for Asia with Japan as enforcer. The secret treaty he created with Japan was never ratified by the Senate of the United States.[lxviii]

President Roosevelt's thinking and actions, without consultation or modification except with Vice-President Taft and a few close others, led to disastrous results for the 20th Century with the re-alignment of world powers and the terrible loss of life in the wars that followed.

Our national Constitution is designed to create checks and balances between three co-equal branches of government called Separation of Powers. It is to prevent one Executive or one Congress or one Supreme Court from acting out of concert with the other branches or to exercise more than co-equal power.

The President can recommend legislation, but Congress passes federal laws; the President can veto a federal law, but Congress can override that veto. The President is Commander in Chief, but Congress declares war; the Senate gives advice and consent to any Treaty that binds the United States, approves all important appointments by the President, and all nominations of Supreme Court Justices. Congress passes federal laws and the President agrees, by oath, to faithfully execute them.

There are not supposed to be any secret treaties; there are not supposed to be executive wars; there is not supposed to be legislation no one can read; there is not supposed to be designed gridlock and tricks of quorum; there are not supposed to be revolutionary concepts rammed through the Courts without republican review. All who serve the public faithfully agree to the spirit and rules of the United States Constitution.

Article II, Section 1

I do solemnly swear (or affirm) that I will faithfully execute the Office of President of the United States, and will to the best of my Ability, preserve, protect and defend the Constitution of the United States.

George Washington added, "So help me God."

Article VI

The Senators and Representatives before mentioned, and the Members of the several State Legislatures, and all executive and judicial Officers, both of the United States and of the several States, shall be bound by Oath or Affirmation, to support this Constitution.

Watching carefully over all this is the Supreme Court of the United States, with its judicial review of federal law and executive action, but always restrained from bypassing, with its decisions, the legislative process meant for the representatives of the people – Congress.

The Supreme Court is never to address Constitutional issues unless all other means of addressing an issue have been thoroughly exhausted. The Court restrains itself and its Justices are subject to being impeached for high crimes and misdemeanors as are all federal officers. In this way, more representatives of the sovereign (the people of the United States) have a say in the discussion of doctrines that can affect the nation for decades or more.[lxix]

Covert actions and secrecy meant to cover up policy also thwarts the 1st Amendment's Free Press Clause whose purpose is to uncover facts and information that give the sovereign accurate information with which to make judgments. The marketplace of facts and interpretations and points of view is meant to create more carefully constructed policy that represents the informed will of the people. An investigatory press is an absolute necessity.

Amendment I, United States Constitution
Congress shall make no law abridging the freedom of the press.

America's taste of imperialism, begun as part of a consolidation of the continent but then expanded, remains not just the leaven of the Pharisees, but an experiment that resulted in millions of lost lives and fractured societies because we entered the world stage at that time with Theodore Roosevelt's questionable judgment and without real knowledge and understanding of what we were doing and the consequences that might occur.

Had the processes put in place by the Supreme Positive Law of our Land been followed, the experiment might not have been made or might have been made in a different way with more wise voices heard before actions were taken. President Roosevelt believed, I'm sure, that most Americans agreed with his foreign policy decisions and I am sure he thought he was doing the right thing. But that sureness, to the Founders in 1787, always needed to be tested in open debate and through the carefully crafted processes they put in place that were ratified by the governed, and which any President has an oath to follow.

Theodore Roosevelt's domestic policies in conservation and "trust-busting," along with his overall popularity, served to embolden his own concept of infallibility in all fields. That is why we have processes that everyone, no matter how sure of their rightness, must follow.

George Washington in his farewell address that was delivered to Congress in writing gave future executives some wise advice about selecting certain nations to favor as Roosevelt had favored Japan.

"A passionate attachment of one Nation for another produces a variety of evils. Sympathy for the favorite nation, facilitating the illusion of an imaginary common interest, in cases where no real common interest exists, and infusing into one the enmities of the other, betrays the former into a participation in the quarrels and Wars of the latter, without adequate inducement or justification... Excessive partiality for one foreign nation and excessive dislike of another, cause those whom they actuate to see danger only on one

side ... we may safely trust to temporary alliances for extraordinary emergencies."[lxx]

10

The Effects in America of the Industrial Revolution

The Progressive Era.

"I had dropped down from the proletariat into what sociologists love to call the 'submerged tenth,' and I was startled to discover the way in which that submerged tenth was recruited. I found there all sorts of men, many of whom had once been as good as myself ... and bodies equal to and better than mine, and which ended there before my eyes in the shambles at the bottom of the Social Pit. And as I listened my brain began to work. I saw the picture of the Social Pit as vividly as though it were a concrete thing, and at the bottom of the Pit I saw them, myself above them, not far, and hanging on to the slippery wall by main strength and sweat. And I confess a terror seized me. I discovered that I was a Socialist. No economic argument affects me as profoundly and convincingly as I was affected on the day when I first saw the walls of the Social Pit rise around me and felt myself slipping down, down, into the shambles at the bottom."[lxxi]

JACK LONDON (1876-1916) FROM *WAR OF THE CLASSES*, 1905

In the 19th century while America was, for the most part, wholly preoccupied within her own expanding borders, Europe was revolutionary, unsettled, and deeply troubled. Whether because of the chaos or for some other reason, some German philosophies ignited in those unsettling times and provided the intellectual case against what they considered the oppression of the Industrial Revolution. These ideas did not reach America immediately but by the end of the century they had a major influence on a segment of American intellectualism and the rise of the private sector labor movement [lxxii]

The era of the Enlightenment, so essential to the United States Constitution, was replaced first by Romanticism, as an emotional reaction to the neo-classicism of the Enlightenment, and second by Idealism as a reaction, in part, to the rising economics of Capitalism. Idealism, as part of some of the German ideologies, means an ideation or idea, not an 'ideal' or personification of perfection.

While certainly not bloodless and not always reasonable, the American Revolution emerged on the world stage with a kind of rational thinking reflected, ultimately, in the United States Constitution of 1787, that gave the whole exercise a kind of luster and myth even if the underlying premise's effectiveness – control of human nature through reasoned structures and processes – remains an open question. America was surprisingly stable.

That stability did not exist with much of Europe through the 19th century beginning with the French Revolution, its bloodbath, and the rise of Napoleon. During this period (1848) Henry David Thoreau wrote:

> *"The progress from an absolute to a limited monarchy, from a limited monarchy to a democracy, is a progress toward a true respect for the individual. Is a democracy, such as we know it, the last improvement possible in government? Is it not possible to take a step further toward recognizing and organizing the rights of man?"[lxxiii]*

One answer to Thoreau came in the person of Karl Marx who posited the alienation of the working person from society and called on the workers of the world to unite in a class struggle, whose ultimate goal was a classless and stateless society of communal living and shared wealth, without private ownership of property.

Progress toward a true respect for the individual, as Thoreau mentions, that further step toward recognizing the rights of man, was intellectually replaced by progress in respecting the group and the rights of the group, in this case the working and peasant classes. Marx, and the many variations of his philosophy, believed that to achieve these goals organization and structure were essential.

Before a society can reach its goal of no government, according to Marx, the role of government is large and overwhelming. The state would take over the means of production and re-distribute the wealth it created. Some of these ideas had been tried on a very small scale in America, mostly coalescing around religious freedom, but with an underlying view of humanity as capable of agreeableness, of mutual cooperation for the common good, and of voluntary personal restraint relative to taking more than one's share.

The followers of Marx hoped for Plockhoy's Commune on a world-wide scale. In 1663, the Dutchman Pieter Cornelius Plockhoy envisioned a welfare society of equality and harmony and established a utopian settlement on the Whorekill clearing near present-day Lewes, Delaware. A year later it was destroyed by Sir Robert Carr as part of his drive to oust the Dutch from New York and the surrounding areas. The Dutch did in fact lose Manhattan to the English just a year later, but this idea of communal harmony lingers invitingly.[lxxiv]

In 1620, William Bradford had also tried this notion of human cooperation in Plymouth and found that just the opposite worked. He reorganized the colony around each family taking care of its own needs first, and ironically, the community began to prosper. This latter philosophic model is what America has adopted, and with boundaries, has worked well.

In competition with Marxist theory, but aligned regarding economic inequality, Anarchists believed that all government is in bed with the wealthy and wanted no part of any organized structure. Unlike the American Founders' view of limited government, the idea was that *all* government was the problem, not the answer to the sufferings of humanity.

The Anarchist Movement terrorized Europe. It disavowed organization and relied on the call to unknown individuals to simply rise up and do their own thing against the current social order. There were newsletters, there were bomb manuals, there were dying statements to the working man to commit acts of terror and take the consequences for the good of the cause. More than seven heads of state and other important persons were brutally murdered. Many more were killed in Russia on behalf of the Peasant Revolution later known as the Bolshevik Revolution of 1917.

1881, Czar Alexander II of Russia, by bomb

1894, President Sadi Carnot of France, by stabbing

1897, Prime Minister Antonio Canovas del Castillo of Spain, shot at close range

1898, Empress Elizabeth of Austria, Queen Consort of Franz Joseph, by dagger

1900, King Humbert of Italy, shot at close range

1901, President William McKinley of the United States, shot at close range

1912, Prime Minister Jose Canalejas of Spain, shot from behind while looking in a bookstore window[lxxv]

There were civilian casualties as well. There were bombs in restaurants, in churches, in the French Parliament and a particularly gruesome bomb went off in a Spanish Opera House that caused several stampeding deaths. In America a manager at Carnegie Steel was shot and stabbed in his office but survived. In Chicago a bomb killed eight policemen and wounded another seventy persons causing fear, panic, and calls for revenge. Eventually, the Anarchist movement gradually disappeared as it resisted organization and structure. In its place Socialist variations rose to prominence and proceeded to work with existing electoral systems and the private labor movement to gain legitimacy.[lxxvi]

Socialism, according to Marx, is a necessary step on the way to this eventual classless society. It took hold to some extent in Europe. In America it was a small but growing political movement based on the new social sciences that promised justification for real societal change. America had reached material and innovative success beyond her wildest dreams. Some citizens were beyond wealthy, and the trusts and corporations and railroads and other big businesses seemed to drive the worker, the little guy, down, down, down, into the Social Pit.

The excesses of the Industrial Revolution were challenged as unjust. In America, this was the Era of the Progressive, a movement that, though changed and morphed with the times, is still very powerful into the 21st century. The emphasis of the Progressives at the turn of the 20th century was not individual rights against state power, or the Liberty Ethic that was so important to the Founders, this was about visions of a better and more equitable society or, as I will call it, the Equality Ethic.

The assumptions about human nature and its negative characteristics that could be checked by religion, virtue, and process according to the Founders, gave way to assumptions about human nature that a large governmental agenda could correct. This agenda would be laid over the public like a blanket and the warmth and comfort of its feel would bring all humankind to more equal status.

The Progressives were working with an Enlightenment inspired federal constitution, with its emphasis on diffused power, but with great energy and vigor they managed to get four Amendments to it ratified between 1913 and 1920 that changed dramatically the relationship between state and local authority relative to federal authority. This is a remarkable achievement considering how hard the Founders deliberately made the Amendment process.

Article V, United States Constitution

The Congress, whenever two thirds of both Houses shall deem it necessary, shall propose Amendments to this Constitution, or, on the Application of the Legislatures of two thirds of the several States, shall call a Convention for proposing Amendments , which, in either Case, shall be valid to all Intents and Purposes, as Part of this Constitution, when ratified by the Legislatures of three fourths of the several States, or by Conventions in three fourths thereof, as the one or the other Mode of Ratification may be proposed by the Congress; Provided that no Amendment which may be made prior to the Year One thousand eight hundred and eight shall in any Manner affect the first and fourth Clauses in the Ninth Section of the first Article; and that no State, without its Consent, shall be deprived of its equal suffrage in the Senate.

These two methods to amend meant that there was genuine public agreement to what was being proposed. Because the Federal Constitution supersedes all state laws and Constitutions, it must have broad appeal. Americans, as sovereign, needed to agree to these changes.

What the early Progressive era clearly shows us is that the 1787 United States Constitution is flexible enough to accommodate real philosophical change and do so in a way that still maintains a stable social order. Profound change occurred but that change was contained within the process of Amendment, as well as through a great deal of innovative legislation passed by Congress. America escaped the social upheaval of the many nations in Europe and Russia in part because the constraints of process were respected by even the most ardent social revolutionaries. Anarchy in America was minimal, though it did reach the level of the Presidency itself when McKinley was assassinated.

Of the four Progressive Era amendments, the first dealt with taxation. Progressives thought that, to fund a more equitable society, a federal income tax was essential. Passed by Congress in 1909, it was ratified in 1913.

Amendment XVI

The Congress shall have power to lay and collect taxes on incomes, from whatever source derived, without apportionment among the several states, and without regard to any census or enumeration.

The wording of this Amendment goes directly to Article I, Section 9 of the Constitution.

No Capitation, or other direct, Tax shall be laid unless in Proportion to the Census or Enumeration herein before directed to be taken

The Effects in America of the Industrial Revolution

The 16th Amendment overturned a Supreme Court ruling that said that taxing income was a "direct" tax and therefore prohibited. The 16th Amendment says that taxing *income* is an acceptable source of revenue for the federal government. Taxing an individual's *wealth* had not been considered by the Founders. However, it was not a new idea in 1913. Progressive (graduated) income tax laws had been passed in several states before the Civil War and even a federal income tax had existed during the Civil War to pay for that cause.

Article I, Section 8 of the Constitution:

The Congress shall have power to lay and collect Taxes, Duties, Imposts and Excises, to pay Debts and provide for the common Defence and general Welfare of the United States ...

The second change was the 17th Amendment which altered the way United States Senators are selected. In lieu of their selection by state legislatures, they now would be popularly elected after open primaries. The 17th Amendment was passed by Congress in 1912 and ratified in 1913.

Amendment XVII

The Senate of the United States shall be composed of two Senators from each State, elected by the people thereof, for six years; and each Senator shall have one vote.

This Amendment eroded the power of each state to select persons to the United States Senate that had a special loyalty to the state and its needs. It also impacted the balance between state and federal power as a horizontal separation of power within the doctrine of Federalism that undergirds our system.

Power shifted to the federal government and away from the states. This issue had been a major topic of discussion at the Constitutional Convention in 1787 which is why the selection process for Senators was adopted by the Convention in the first place. In the debates regarding the proposed Constitution, the Anti-federalists screamed loudly that national power would prevail, ultimately, and open the door to the tyranny they were trying to prevent.

The idea of social reform begun by the Progressives has always seen the federal government as the organ of such reform. Each state has had its reform movements, but the thrust of large social change was seen as having to come from Congress and applied universally across the nation. At the turn of the 20th century the sting of Southern-state defiance in the mid-19th century still hung in the air, and many thought that social justice would come as a result of legislation from the federal government. The 17th Amendment, then, made the possibility of federal Progressive legislation more probable.

The third major change, the 18th Amendment, is a pure Progressive-era idea of how, with one action, to mitigate the immense social problems commensurate with alcohol. These problems were acute in the West where saloons and negative behaviors associated with them affected the basis of society, namely the family. This Amendment was proposed in 1917 and ratified in 1919. This action might be the poster child of benign intent and unintended consequences.

Amendment XVIII

After one year from the ratification of this article the manufacture, sale, or transportation of intoxicating liquors within, the importation thereof into, or the exportation thereof from the United States and all territory subject to the jurisdiction thereof for beverage purposes is hereby prohibited.

The 18th Amendment was repealed by the 21st Amendment. The National Woman's Christian Temperance Union was nevertheless a big deal and many states and counties passed Blue Laws restricting the sale of alcohol or prohibiting it entirely after the repeal. From their declaration of principles in 1902:

"[We] declare our purpose to educate the young; to form a better public sentiment; to reform so far as possible, by religious, ethical, and scientific means, the drinking classes; to seek the transforming power of Divine Grace for ourselves and all for whom we work, that

they and we may willfully transcend no law of pure and wholesome living; and finally we pledge ourselves to labor and to pray that all of these principles, founded on the Gospel of Christ, may be worked out into the customs of society and the laws of the land."[lxxvii]

19th - vote

The fourth change, the Susan B. Anthony Amendment, as it was called, the 19th Amendment took decades to pass but enfranchised more persons in one fell swoop than the original enfranchisement of white and later of black American males. It was the West that really pushed this notion as women were such a precious commodity that perhaps showing them some intellectual respect might just lure them to the female-starved West. Four western states led the way with Wyoming, Colorado, Utah, and Idaho giving women the vote. It was written and proposed in 1878 and ratified in 1920.

Amendment XIX

The right of citizens of the United States to vote shall not be denied or abridged by the United States or by any State on account of sex.

The four Progressive Amendments might be a simple modification after one hundred years of growth and industrial expansion after the American Revolution. Problems not anticipated in an agrarian and merchant society needed attention. It was a major power shift, however, from state to national power that has grown exponentially ever since. It was also a shift in emphasis from Liberty to Equality.

"Human institutions can be changed, but man cannot: whatever may be the general endeavor of a community to render its members equal and alike, the personal pride of individuals will always seek to rise above the line, to form somewhere an inequality to their own advantage. In aristocracies, men are separated from each other by lofty stationary barriers: in democracies, they are divided by many small and almost invisible threads, which are constantly broken or moved from place to place. Thus, whatever may be the progress of equality, in democratic nations a great number of small private

Apples of Gold

associations will always be formed within the general pale of society."

ALEXIS DE TOCQUEVILLE, 1831[lxxviii]

The Progressive Amendments also represent a significant break relative to the way people see reality, and it is this break that constitutes part of the cultural angst we are experiencing into the 21st century. Are there, as the Founders would have maintained, objective truths around which to organize society or is reality subjective, hence no fixed organizing principles exist?

Our senses and experience tell us things over time. If we cannot rely on our senses and we discount experience as era-relevant, accepted notions about the nature of human beings and various attempts at effectively harnessing the good and constraining the bad melt away as illusory as the very truth of the senses and empiricism are questioned. In some ways this may account for the myriad of philosophical tides and experiments we take as a nation as *ideas* and *ideologies* come in and out of fashion about the best systems for statecraft and governance of an ever moving object – the nature of humanity itself.

Some of these ideas were made Amendments to the United States Constitution and went through the rigorous process of public acceptance. Some of these ideas, freely expressed in our open "marketplace of ideas," raise nothingness to an objective truth. Some of these ideas raise science to the sacred and deny any essential unprovable element in human nature. Some of these ideas create, through technology, the ability for human beings to invent inviting ways to de-humanize people and eventually do away with them altogether.[lxxix]

We are now past the Industrial Revolution and into the Technological Revolution. Technology has outpaced philosophy and we are trying to deal with it with a few rules and crossed fingers. If you see a child under four years old with a hand-held computer, you are watching a child at risk because we do not know the long-term effect of this technology on his or her humanity.

The Effects in America of the Industrial Revolution

What genius is now emerging from childhood with yet another philosophical notion on the nature of truth and reality that we might want to take seriously? Why wouldn't these new ideations simply sweep the United States Constitution out of the way as one pulls down remnants of history that were once significant and now monuments meant to teach and remind or simply cast away as not comporting to a current way of thinking?

The Founders accepted certain universals about human behavior that guided the structure they created whose purpose was to establish justice, insure domestic tranquility, provide for the common defense, promote the general welfare, and secure the blessings of liberty to themselves and their progeny. They also accepted the notion that human beings have natural rights and that God is the author of these rights. They were all about the individual and "progress toward a true respect for the individual" under the auspices of a Supreme Being to whom everyone owes a duty.

The idea that individuals respond to the local and the close at hand was altered at the turn of the 20th century and we are in the process of finding out if some of that alteration was wise or not.

Part III

E PLURIBUS UNUM

From many, one

11

The Yellow Bus

Education as a goal and a glue.

The wheels on the bus go round and round
Round and round; round and round
The wheels on the bus go round and round
All through the town.

A CHILDREN'S SONG – VERNA HILLS, 1939

T he ubiquitous school bus -- always yellow, always stopping, always putting out a little flag to tell us children might be crossing the street, and always doing this at exactly the wrong time for our hurried lives. If the bus were ever painted a different color no one could be held responsible for what would happen across this nation. But it is an official color – *school bus yellow*— and what began as a *kid's hack* or horse-drawn farm wagon, became the symbol of public education in America.

Education is one of the unifying aspects of life in America, not because education today unites us, but simply because it is universally required. New England took the lead. The great migration of 1630 to the Massachusetts Bay Colony and the Puritan lifestyle included the establishment of common schools as early as 1642. Higher education was also a priority. Ministers were needed for the influx coming into the Colony to lead them on the proper pathway to salvation and good order and peace. Harvard was first — proposed in 1633 and chartered in 1650. William and Mary, chartered in 1693, with Yale following in 1701.

Typical of what higher education consisted of in the colonies is described in the statutes of the College of William and Mary in Virginia:

"In the Philosophy School we appoint two masters ... one of these masters shall teach rhetoric, logic, and ethics, the other physics, metaphysics, and mathematics. And that the youth of the college may the more cheerfully apply themselves to these studies and endeavor to rise to the academic degrees, we do, according to the form and institution of the two famous universities in England, allot four years before they attain to the degree of Bachelor, and seven years before they attain the degree of Master of Arts."[lxxx]

These universities, of course, were for children of the relatively well-to-do who had previously sent their children back to England for further education after being privately tutored at home. That these early American colleges came into existence and were funded after a relatively brief period of colonial survival and development is testament to the importance of literacy to Protestant Americans who placed great value on reading or following the Scriptures.

Primary education was a different matter. We can see right away the difference in commitment between New England and the South due partly to the more tight-knit nature of New England communities and strict governance structures.

The 1642 Massachusetts Bay Colony records state:

"Forasmuch as the good education of children is of singular behoof and benefit to any commonwealth, and whereas many parents and masters are too indulgent and negligent of their duty in that kind: It is ordered that the selectmen of every town shall have a vigilant eye over their brethren and neighbors to see, first, that none of them shall suffer so much barbarism in any of their families as not to endeavor to teach, by themselves or others, their children and apprentices so much learning as may enable them perfectly to read the English tongue and knowledge of capital laws, upon penalty for each neglect therein."[lxxxi]

Plymouth Colony soon followed and applied profits from its fisheries to build schools.[1]

In the South, specifically Virginia, 1646, however:

"Whereas sundry laws have established for the better educating of youth in honest and profitable trades and manufactures, as also to avoid sloth and idleness wherewith such young children are easily corrupted that justices of the peace should, at their discretion, bind out children to tradesmen or husbandmen to be brought up in some good and lawful calling. [but] forasmuch as for the most part the parents are most averse and unwilling to part with their children Be it therefore enacted that the commissioners of the several counties make choice of two children in each county of the age of eight or seven years, either male or female, which are to be sent up to James City, to be employed in the public flax houses." [lxxxii]

In the colonies south of New England (New York, New Jersey, Pennsylvania, Delaware, and Maryland) one-half of all immigrants came under contract. Orphans from Europe were sent by the shipload to be apprenticed for seven years or until age twenty-four for boys and twenty-one for girls or marriage, whichever came first. After their apprenticeships they were typically given acreage, tools, food, and housing for a year so that they could establish their own lives. This system caused severe labor shortages as many of the newly un-apprenticed would rather have starved to death on their own land than work for wages for their former master. They built isolated homesteads that were hard for communities to defend and many pioneer homesteads were lost to native-American attack for this reason.

Whether in the North or South, the children of slaves were seldom sent to official schools, but some were taught by kindly mistresses, other children, or by ministers so the Bible could be read, and souls saved. Northern Quakers were especially helpful in teaching basic reading, writing, and sums to slave and free-black children. Many found a way to learn to read and write from each other. Sometimes, though rarely, a slave in the South might be educated for the purposes of record keeping for the plantation. Lack of literacy was also true for many poorer or apprenticed white colonial children, especially girls.

In 1753, Benjamin Franklin wrote humorously about the many attempts to educate native-American youth. An offer was made during peace negotiations to take six native-Americans and educate them through college. The elders of the tribes discussed the proposal and made their decision.

> *"The Indians, after consulting on the proposals, replied that it was remembered that some of their youths had formerly been educated at that college, but that it had been observed that for a long time after they returned to their friends, they were absolutely good for nothing – being neither acquainted with the true methods of killing deer, catching beavers, or surprising an enemy. The proposition they looked on, however, as a mark of kindness and goodwill of the English to the Indian nations, which merited a grateful return; and, therefore, if the English gentlemen would send a dozen or two of their children to Onondago, the Great Council would take care of their education, bring them up in what was really the best manner, and make men of them."*[lxxxiii]

Education in America has always been seen in several different ways, those ways emphasized by different proponents for different reasons. Almost all thinkers, writers, theologians, philosophers, would-be intellectuals, and some parents, thought education in some form an important part of one's relationship with Scripture and part of a system for individual economic or marital advancement.

Much later, almost all Americans thought the benefits, relative to each of their points of view, should be extended to both genders and all races and backgrounds. Today, American public education is extended to anyone within the jurisdiction of a state, including those here illegally, if that state provides public education. Public education is a state (not a federal) fundamental right if the state provides for that right in its state Constitution.[lxxxiv]

Colonial higher education emphasized the classics, the dead languages of Greek and Latin, and moral philosophy and theology. While the ordinary person needed to be able to read the Scriptures on his or her own, it was also thought that the ordinary person needed learned and virtuous interpreters to lessen the inclination to sin and broaden the inclination to goodness. Harvard, William and Mary, and Yale were founded to further John Winthrop's idea of America as the shining City on a Hill. In other words, to keep America as a Christian nation, whose moral law is Judeo-Christian, whose founding, according to William Bradford, amounted to a covenant with God.

As colonists survived and strengthened their hold on America in the 17th and early 18th centuries, religion, although very important in theory, seemed to show some signs of weakening. The very separation that William Bradford was so worried about between the individual and his duties to God seemed to increase in direct relationship to affluence and progress and the rise of individualism within the colonies. It would take a very cold, freezing dose of reality to bring the colonists back in line with the original covenant.

That dose of reality came in the form of George Whitefield and what is known as the Great Awakening of Calvinist religious thought in America between approximately 1720 and 1740. George Washington was born in this period. A Methodist, George Whitefield came to America and preached invigorating, stirring, wrenching, sermons in the genre of Jonathan Edwards. These sermons revived evangelical Christianity. More ministers were needed; more colleges were formed, some of which were not associated with the training of ministers: Princeton in 1746, Brown in 1764, Rutgers in 1766, Dartmouth in 1769, and the University of Pennsylvania in 1740. Benjamin Franklin proposed a secular University of Pennsylvania in 1749 that was chartered in 1755.

For the colonists in the non-coastal (non-plantation) areas of the South the shining city began to tarnish quickly and the stabilizing effects of literacy and possibly higher education at William and Mary simply did not exist. What would it be like for one of those orphans or one of those paupers sent to a master to learn a trade in America?

Perhaps your parents did love you but died in the cesspool of disease that was Europe in the 17th and 18th centuries. Perhaps your impoverished parents had no choice but to send you and your brothers and sisters away. Perhaps your mother died of infection in childbirth leaving eight or nine siblings and your father could not take care of you.

These factors also influenced some of the children who came as slaves but with the added danger of simply being snatched up by traders going inland to find more and more slaves to ship west at the height of the African slave trade.

The orphans from Europe received clothes and food and passage on a ship to America along with a myriad of other children. The ones who were lucky got a master who was relatively kind and took time to teach them the rudiments of reading and writing. In every case they had to live through many years of apprenticeship until they were old enough to win their liberty. Think what this must have been like. Some children just died; some went inward; some got mean; some decided to make the best of it and see what they could do.

If you were a boy and twenty-one and lived on an isolated farm in the interior South as an orphan-apprentice, you eventually got a start as your own master. You must have had the grit to survive having been through what you later might have had to suppress as too painful to describe. This is how the system created new colonists where endless empty lands existed with not enough human beings to tame and cultivate it. These boys married and went to the back country where they could stake a claim to liberty and property of their own. The dream of every feudal serf and tenant farmer over time immemorial to own their own land was accomplished in America.

Not all the emigrants were poor. Those with some money wanted to stay on the coast where the "civilized" lived and where, if their skills were mercantile, a relatively stable life could be created. These were whole families with furniture and linen and a Bible who thought there were economic opportunities in the New World. Quickly, the difference in life between the coastal elite and the interior poor began to take shape, and what we describe as the civilizing Rule of Law, applied unevenly, began to erode the social fabric of the South and smash the dream so costly won.

As the Reverend Charles Woodmason describes in 1764:

"Our large stocks of cattle are ... stolen and all our horses ... carried off. Houses have been burned ... and families stripped and turned naked into the woods... Married women have been ravished,

virgins deflowered, and other unheard of cruelties committed by these barbarous ruffians ... being let loose by the magistrates ..For, instead of public justice ... such have been let loose among us to repeat their villainies and strip us of the few remaining cattle, horses, and movables which, after their former visits they had left us. [B]ack country inhabitants travel 200-300 miles ... to prosecute offenders ... attend the courts ... even to spending their last shilling ... to defray their traveling and town costs. After which they are obliged to trudge home on foot ... The juries of every court are generally composed of the inhabitants of Charleston, persons who know not even the geography, much less the persons and concerns of the back country. What church can we repair to for divine service? For the common people hardly know the first principles of religion; and so corrupt are their morals among them that a reformation in manners in our time is more to be wished for than expected. [lxxxv]

The romantic notion many came with of personal rights as a British citizen equally applied in early America. The notion of law and order, of a utopia of simple Christian living, of reading Scripture, was more a cauldron of advantage, disadvantage, outrage, brutality, and all the commensurate qualities in human behavior that, mixed together in the boiling liquid of life, sometimes reduce human beings to their basest elements.

Reverend Woodmason continues,

"[A] great multitude of children are now grown up in the greatest ignorance of everything save vice, in which they are adept. Consequently, they lead idle and immoral lives, for they, having no sort of education, naturally follow ... every species of wickedness."

We have the writings of Reverend Woodmason because he sent long letters to the political powers of colonial South Carolina hoping for a redress for these grievances. Amid all this carnage in non-coastal areas, he still thought the right thing to do was to plead for help in a civilized way. What the back-country colonists thought was the right thing to do was to create lawless "regulator associations" to take matters of justice into their own hands and some began to feel a kind of superiority in illiteracy. Many kids were regularly tutored at home, especially in the more prosperous cities, but in the back country, schools were scarce to non-existent, with itinerant instructors and irregular sessions.

It cannot be emphasized enough that America was a British colony and looked to Europe for guidance in things of refinement, of taste, of education. We were British with new experiences in the wilderness, but we were British. It was the British who elevated intellectual prowess; it was the British with fine arts and literature; it was the British with the new energy of the industrial revolution.

And what were we? We were adventurers into a new realm of reality. The heart and soul of these adventurers were Christians looking for a new place to live out their beliefs without the religious persecutions prevalent in Europe. These adventurers were for the most part not titled and not part of the ancient governing class. They were simple products of the Protestant Reformation who had risked life and limb and loneliness and starvation to put into the practice of daily living their strongly held beliefs, including how they educated their surviving children. That education was uneven to say the least.

America is a compendium of experiences, each one unique, each one deserving of attention, but none the definition of what the American experience is. We say the Scottish Enlightenment; we say the French Enlightenment; we say the British Enlightenment; we say the German Reformation; but we don't say any of these things about America. That is because we are not one thing, with one preferred taste, with one intellectual reality, with a particular form of art, one national idea of music, with a few signature geniuses who personify the national identity, with one anything except the idea of being one Western nation under God, indivisible, with the symbols we chose as unifiers of our national life.

I have chosen the yellow school bus as one of those symbols but what goes on in those buses and in those schools is not consistent, even though there are standards. The experience is very individual because New

Mexico is not Massachusetts; Alaska is not Florida; Hawaii is not New Jersey. Catholic kids are not Amish kids; Mormon kids are not Presbyterian kids; Muslim kids are not Genizaros kids; Hopi kids are not Gullah/Geechee kids. Distinctions are recognized and practiced in public schools all over the nation even though over many decades we have gradually homogenized.

In 1925, the Supreme Court ruled that while the states can require that children go to school, they cannot require that they go to public schools. The government is not allowed, it ruled, to take the ultimate decision of educating children out of the hands of the parents who have a duty to guide the development of the child. So, while we have standards, parents can home-school their children; they can send their children to parochial schools that include religious education; they can send their kids to private schools or public charter schools. If Amish, parents can end their children's public education experience earlier than other groups. Our model is not the European model where kids are selected to move on or are barred from going in a certain direction unless they pass certain exams. [lxxxvi]

Although our K-12 system is uniquely American, our early higher education emulated the best practices in Britain. In the 1700s new and important institutions emerged such as King's College (1754), later Columbia University, and Rhode Island Baptist College, later Brown University. We also became interested in the practical and in scientific inquiry establishing the Philosophical Society of Philadelphia, the American Academy of Arts and Sciences, the Pennsylvania Society for the Encouragement of Manufacturers and Useful Arts, just around the time of the American Revolution and the Constitution of 1787.

But these institutions did not represent America; they represented *some* of America. Some of America was still in the back country of South Carolina, North Carolina, and Georgia trying to survive with irregular basic education in reading and writing and sums. Some of America was still bound in legal servitude with no formal education at all although literacy was highly prized in this community.

Thomas Jefferson's educational model encompassed both European and American realities and was embraced by many. He thought we needed to educate everyone in the basics and then select the gifted to continue. The highly gifted he believed should receive free university educations. What that university education consisted of was the development of the classical mind and the scientific mind for the purpose of enriching, enhancing, and progressing society. Since any society has only so many geniuses, Jefferson thought these persons must be carefully identified and educated. The emphasis, then, was the good of society not the fulfillment of "self" as it is today.

The Age of Enlightenment philosophy, upon which our federal Constitution is based, and upon which our earliest views of higher education are based, slipped away quietly in the 19th century into Romanticism and into German Idealism. These new ideations entered the sphere of education in a big way in America in the forms of Johann Herbart (1776-1841) and J.H. Pestalozzi (1746-1827). Both emphasized the elevation of the development of truth *as the child sees* it, not as the parent sees it, or as society sees it. This and the other ideas and manifestations of it became the philosophy of John Dewey and others whose influence on American primary education is enormous. It is known as the Doctrine of Progressive Education.

Francis Parker, a famous educational innovator at the Cook County Normal School in Chicago expressed the idea in the late 19th century:

> *"I believe the only consistency in this world worthy the name is constant change in the direction of a better knowledge of humanity and of the means by which humanity rises to higher levels ... the march of progress is upon the line of the realization of infinite possibilities for the good and growth of mankind...The future of education means the closest study and diagnosis of each personality and the application of means to develop that personality in to the highest stature of manhood or womanhood.. I believe in universal salvation on earth through education."[lxxxvii]*

John Dewey (1859-1952), an American philosopher, organized an experimental elementary school at the University of Chicago. In an address given in 1899, he reflected on the impact of the Industrial Revolution:

The Yellow Bus

"The obvious fact is that our social life has undergone a thorough and radical change. If our education is to have any meaning for life, it must pass through an equally complete transformation... Those modifications of our school system are in reality signs and evidences of evolution ... the change in the moral school atmosphere, in the relation of pupils and teachers – of discipline ... all these are not mere accidents; they are necessities of the larger social evolution . . .To do this means to make each one of our schools an embryonic community life...we shall have a larger society which is worthy, lovely, and harmonious."[lxxxviii]

The importance of the rise and elevation of Progressive ideas, the virtually universal acceptance of natural selection in the human species as outlined by Charles Darwin in *The Origin of Species in 1859,* and the introduction of industrialization in the West, led to the idea of the certainty of human progress and therefore the need for an educational system that reflected this progress.

Instead of God, the center of all became *man*, whether as a child or as an adult. Education, which had previously been viewed as a practical tool for existence, a laboratory for the truly intellectually gifted, or a platform for the training of moral virtue and duty, now became a collective incubator for the common good and the new ideas of human progress in fashion at the time. These ideas were to be delivered by the public school. As Dewey said, *"Here [in America] individualism and socialism are at one."*

In loco parentis became obsolete. The primacy of parental control and guidance became obsolete. The development of the classical mind (liberal education) became obsolete. Ideology, the subjective, not information, the objective *"general knowledge"* as John Locke put it, became standardized education for American students. We have been experimenting with our children's education for some time now and the dismal results speak for themselves. There is no solid footing. The history of Western Civilization, in detail, is not being taught so we are left to wander into an unsure "new" without the timeless anchors to steady the movement forward.

An example of this might be in the arena of economics. The notion of descent and conveyance (ownership that is transferred from one generation to another) is at the heart of Western prosperity. Something can be privately owned in the first place, an unalienable right to John Locke, developed by one generation, and value added with the next generation and thereafter. For those societies for whom everything is collective, there is no private ownership and therefore no descent and conveyance. There would be no need for surveys, deeds, Wills, or evidence of private ownership that could be conveyed and hopefully improved generation after generation. Every child living in our system needs to know how this works.

In addition to objective information, the social organization of America, undergirded by the family unit, accepted prior to the ideations of Progressive education, certain universal truths about human beings and their behavior that begins with the notion that man is not a mere species but a reflection of the divine and owes a duty to his or her Creator and a humility about his or her gifts relative to his or her failings. Children owe a duty to their parents, to their teachers and those that help shape and guide them.

Self-actualization, known as personal liberty in our system, begins with duty and is a gradually developed process from childhood to adulthood. There is no such thing as equality in America outside the concept of fair and impartial treatment within the Rule of Law, called equal protection of the law. The law is not the same for children as it is for adults. Children do not have the biological ability to grasp some abstractions and do not fully develop until sometime in their twenties.

We see the results in both primary and secondary education, as the "march of progress" links itself with current unsubstantiated ideations about human beings and their behavior and bypasses, for the most part, a required and deep study into roots, and wisdom from prior experience, and objective information that are essential for sovereign citizens to know.

In order for *e pluribus unum* to have real meaning, all Americans and other children living here must learn the philosophies, the history (with all the mistakes and moral failings), the economics, the civics, the traditions, the expectations, the duties, the rights against government, and the virtues that create a stable social order in which they are to grow, develop and prosper. These things do not come in and out of fashion and they cannot be bypassed or forgotten over the generations without danger to the social order itself.

This common understanding, meticulously learned from one generation to the next is what represents the *unum* in our society and is added to each child's individual familial cultural experience, of whatever variety, that represents the huge melting pot that is America. This learning through the English language is how we become Americans from different places all over the world.

In 1895, the Roman Catholic Bishop, John Spalding, in emphasizing the need for parochial in addition to public education, added other essentials to the education process:

> *"The truly human is found not in knowledge alone but also in faith, in hope, in love, in pure-mindedness, in reverence, in the sense of beauty, in devoutness, in the thrill of awe, which Goethe says is the highest thing in man."[lxxxix]*

At the turn of the 20th century, before traditional education was all but abandoned, many immigrant children and their parents held our system of primary education in such high regard they could hardly breathe.

> *"In America, then, everything was free, as we had heard in Russia. Light was free; the streets were as bright as a synagogue on a holy day ... Education was free...the essence of American opportunity, the treasure that no thief could touch, not even misfortune or poverty. A little girl from across the alley came and offered to conduct us to school ... this child, who had never seen us until yesterday, who could not pronounce our names, who was not much better dressed than we, was able to offer us the freedom of the schools of Boston! No application made, no questions asked, no examinations, rulings, exclusions, no machinations, no fees. The doors stood open for every one of us. The smallest child could show*

us the way... So, it was with a heart full of longing and hope that my father led us to school on that first day... At last the four of us stood around the teacher's desk; and my father, in his impossible English, gave us over in her charge, with some broken word of his hopes for us that his swelling heart could no longer contain. "[xc]

MARY ANTIN, AN IMMIGRANT CHILD, 1912

One of the most difficult tasks of any society is how to "modernize" without losing all. From our earliest moments as inhabitants of a New World the American people have believed deeply in some form of public education. The notion has been around for four hundred years, but what we are teaching our children in those schools, more importantly, what we are *not* teaching in those schools, may undermine the very hard work and precious assets that went into creating them. For the very poor and struggling New England farmer in 1642 to Mary Antin's father, arriving first without his family in 1912, the long hours and mind-numbing work that went into paying their share of school tax were worth it.

"The wheels on the bus go round and round
Round and round; round and round
The wheels on the bus go round and round
All through the town."

12

A Diverse Culture

Influenced by but not European.

"In music our [America's] problem was a special one ... our elders came home [from Europe] full of admiration for the treasures of European musical art...and their identification with it ... made the seeking out of any other art formula a kind of sacrilege. The artist should feel himself affirmed and buoyed up by his community. Art and the life of art must mean something in the deepest sense, to the everyday citizen."[xci]

AARON COPLAND (1900-1990) AMERICAN COMPOSER,

FROM HIS BOOK *MUSIC AND IMAGINATION:*

Art, in all its forms, affirms and buoys up the community. Emigrants brought with them memories and idolizations of long-recognized European music, dance, art, literature, and poetry and other art forms. West Africans brought the same memories of their music and dance. But there were no artistic standards in America that any European would recognize. Bluegrass in its earliest forms did not count. The theater did not really take off until the time of the Revolution and the presentations were mostly of European works. We had our poets and authors, but none were seen as equivalent to the masters of Europe.

Unknown and unappreciated by both American colonists and European sophisticates was the fact that we did have complex indigenous dance through native-American traditions. Through dance tribes were worshipping, imploring, honoring, and expressing a connection to human life and all living things. Sometimes preparing for war and sometimes hoping for rain, there is a heartbeat in these dances through drums that is compelling.

Later, African influences in rhythm, syncopation, pulse, sway, eroticism, and invention soaked into the culture and the bloodstream of America in a unique way. These influences altered traditional European expressions and formed original, authentic American dance. You know these forms as the Charleston, the Jitterbug, the Shag, and every year or so yet another representation of this massive contribution emerges in American culture.

Our roots are also Separatist and Puritan. What would William Bradford, John Winthrop, and John Cotton have thought? They would not have thought highly of any art form that elevated the sensuous in any regard. English village dancing did evolve in pre-Revolutionary America. George Washington himself was an avid and sought-after dancer. But it was not until the mid-19th century that serious ballet visited the United States. The Metropolitan Opera was not formed until 1880, the Juilliard School of Music not until 1905. We have never come close to the unsurpassed Russian ballet of Pavlova and Nijinsky.

Slowly, non-native American dance creativity emerged in the form of Martha Graham and her ingenious techniques, and many others before and after her. The human body as a musical instrument had never been thought of that way before her performances.

Katherine Dunham, brilliant scholar at the University of Chicago, and founder of the Negro Dance Group and creator of anthropological dance from her extensive studies in the Caribbean and South America. The dance genius of Michael Jackson and others is uniquely American. The gift from God of Philadelphian Marian Anderson's voice cannot be appreciated enough and her many years spent touring in Europe, our country's loss.

In many cultures art forms are a part of what brings identity and pride to a whole people. This is simply not true in the United States. America's geniuses are recognized and appreciated by knowing segments of society or states and in prestigious intellectual bodies, but their touch is a tap on the shoulder here, not a warm embrace. Typical of the view of the

American artist is given in a speech by Sinclair Lewis in Sweden upon accepting the Nobel Prize in Literature in 1930:

> *"The only arts that are vital and respected [in America] are architecture and film ... America with her wealth and power, has not yet produced a civilization good enough to satisfy the deepest wants of human creatures ... The American novelist or poet or dramatist or sculptor or painter ... is oppressed by something worse than poverty – by the feeling that what he creates does not matter, that he is expected to be ... only a decorator or a clown ... America has never had a [Georg] Brandes, a [Hippolyte] Taine, a [Johann Wolfgang von] Goethe, and [Benedetto] Croce ... It is my fate to swing constantly from optimism to pessimism and back, but so is it the fate of anyone who writes or speaks of anything in America – the most contradictory, the most depressing, the most stirring, of any land in the world today."[xcii]*

What is it that we can say, then, represents a cultural unifier America? What is one of those somethings that one might put a finger on and find a pulse common to the nation? We know it is not a tap on the shoulder in the arts, fine and otherwise, nor is it religion, however rooted we are in trying to understand the appropriate purposes of our lives. We have been conditioned, now, to relegate the whole subject to the private and personal conscience of everyone rather than have religion as central to the organized organic nature of our country. However, comforting it is to hear the bells and other calls to worship, that comfort remains tightly retained, or at most only paused over, as we move on in our thoughts to the now and not the hereafter.

It could be the fireworks on the 4th of July that John Adams recommended in 1777 and are a part of our holiday traditions that commemorate our independence as a whole nation. It could be our flag or national anthem, but these have become forms of symbolic speech that are often politicized in such a way that honoring them creates division rather than unification.

There is, however, at least one uniting feature of the American landscape, though not considered artistic and certainly undisciplined, and that is the parade – a simple, long or short, small town American Parade. First, a parade is sheer organization. A sign must go up in multiple places saying that certain roads will be closed from a certain time on a certain day. Detours must be established. This notice alone induces the anticipatory. Rain or shine; cold or hot, it all takes place in a remarkably primitive choreography of a kind Martha Graham would appreciate. Chairs are set out on the curb, undisturbed, by the veteran watcher.

Behind it all is a mysterious organization of volunteers, public servants, school band directors, veteran's groups, Girl Scouts, Boy Scouts, after-school clubs, antique car owners, quarter-horse riding clubs, Llama breeders, farmers with tractors, big shiny trucks, fire engines, parental guides, instruments of all kinds, princes and princesses, Santa and Mrs. Claus and his helpers or a Pilgrim boy and girl, or a Drum and Fife Corps, or Miss Daffodil, dogs and their owners in matching outfits, puppies in a wagon, floats, boats of every description, sound equipment on a flatbed at full volume, Scots in kilts, the Irish in hats, the Union Gospel Singers in crisp white shirts and black pants, flags and color guards, baton throwers, service clubs, Shriner's tiny cars weaving in and out, John Philip Sousa's "Stars and Stripes Forever," wrapped candy, smiles, waves, holiday songs, all ages, all races, all conditions, all feeling the same good will, tapping and singing if they recognize the song, a special "hello" and recognition from one of the elves to a friend on the corner, the hand on the heart of some as the American flag goes by, a hat removed, a salute given, the earnest faces of the band members as they try to keep a straight line in step with the unrelenting drums.

Somehow they all gather on time, most keep up with the group in front of them, sort of, the Chief of Police leading the way with his lights on waving to those he serves, whose deputy pulls up the rear to let everyone know the roads will soon be passable. Some form of a small-town parade goes on all over America, with each region having its special and unique cultural representation. Not every parade has a marching unit in authentic costumes from the War of 1812 but St. Michaels, Maryland does.

The small-town American Parade is short; it is not intellectual. It binds for a second and then releases each person back into his or her peculiar and very individual life, just like the bells in a New England village church reminding us to present ourselves. Sinclair Lewis was talking about artistic standards with the implication that Europe has them and America does not. He saw literature, poetry and art as social binders to British, French, German, Scandinavian, Italian, and Spanish cultures across the pond. He also implied that America in 1930 was not sophisticated enough to be called "civilized." He might be challenged about intellectual standards in traditional art, but is there not a type of art in the innately binding little parade that reminds the ardent individualist that is an American of his or her communal associations, duties, and tolerances?

It is important to distinguish the American Parade from another unifier and that is the American March. A parade is a cultural binder and community builder; a march is a Federal Constitutional right.

The United States Constitution, Amendment I:

Congress shall make no law...abridging...the freedom of speech ...or the right of the people peaceably to assemble, and to petition the Government for a redress of grievances.

A march is a type of speech and assembly. It is symbolic speech. A parade is a type of love. The parade emerges from the community and represents what the community feels is important. It might be history; it might be the social commitments that the community supports; it might be a way to show-case the school band or chorus; it might be any number of things that over time have become important locally and it is locally that the traffic or other public safety issues are handled.

On the other hand, a march is often about a political or social issue or issues that a group of citizens wish to bring to the attention of state or national political leaders. It is fully protected from government interference, with reasonable restrictions, if the restrictions do not go to the content of the speech, symbolic or otherwise.

What does this really mean? This means that what is "hate speech" to one group is not hate speech to another, as Associate Justice Harlan told us in 1971. It means that hostile reactions to political speech do not justify government interference with it. It means that any government actors, whether they are from tax-supported universities or public authorities from towns, cities, and counties must protect the speaker in their professional roles whether they agree with the views expressed.[xciii]

This concept of "free speech" is unique to America. We proclaimed, by ratifying the United States Constitution and vowing always to preserve, protect, and defend it, that the marketplace of ideas is one of the essential components of personal liberty. We proclaimed through the United States Supreme Court that no government actor can prescribe what shall be orthodox in politics or religion or any other matter of opinion and we proclaimed that no official, school administrator, or anyone else in authority can force any citizen to believe or confess to believe in any particular viewpoint.

In practical terms we are required to support views we abhor in the interests of free political thought and free expression of this type of thought within reasonable limits. Free expression of political thought does not include obscenity; it does not include rude violations of unwritten law; it does not include inciting imminent fear that no counter speech can affect; and it never includes violence or law breaking. One can be hateful in the right forum under the right restrictions but can never be rude. This is a unique concept in the world.

Those who hold political and or social views that one disagrees with are called upon to counter those views with others. The March, as well as the Parade, are unifiers in America as we are one of the few remaining nations that support free, polite, non-obscene express, symbolic, or proxy speech in a public forum on public policy issues within reasonable time, place, and manner restrictions, whether the majority of citizens agree with the content of the speech or not. The word "reasonable" does not include excessive security fees that amount to suppression of speech by bankrupting the resources of a person or group. The parade makes us smile; the march makes us think. Both, ironically, are part of the *unum* of America that is hard for some to understand.

"I have worked, boys, I have worked with you for years. I have seen the suffering children, and in order to be convinced I went into the mines on the night shift and day shift and helped the poor wretches to load coal at times ... I have worked in the factories of Georgia and Alabama, and these bloodhounds were tearing the hands off of children and working them 14 hours a day ... Go down, men of today, who rob and exploit, go down into hell and look at the ruins you have put there ... Now my boys ... we have marched together, but I can see victory in the Heavens for you ... We must redeem the world ... I talked with a mother who had her small children working. She said to me, 'Mother, they are not of age, but I had to say they were; I had to tell them they were of age so they could get a chance to help me to get something to eat ... I put [the savings] into a cow and we had some milk for the little ones.'"[xciv]

"MOTHER" JONES,
A POPULAR LABOR LEADER ON BEHALF OF MINERS, 1912

"I believe in God who made of one blood all races that dwell on earth. I believe that all men, black and brown and white, are brothers ... alike in soul and in the possibility of infinite development. Especially do I believe in the Negro Race; in the beauty of its genius, the sweetness of its soul, and its strength in that meekness which shall yet inherit this turbulent Earth. ... I believe in the Devil and his angels, who wantonly work to narrow the opportunity of struggling human beings, especially if they be black; who spit in the faces of the fallen, strike them that cannot strike again, believe the worst and work to prove it, hating the image which is their maker stamped on a Brother's soul."[xcv]

W.E.B. DU BOIS,
ON BEHALF OF AFRICAN AMERICANS, 1904

"President after President has appointed commission after commission to inquire into and report upon Indian affairs. The reports are filled with eloquent statements of wrongs done to the

Apples of Gold

Indians, or perfidies on the part of the Government. These reports are bound up with the Government's Annual Reports, and that is the end of them. However great perplexity and difficulty there may be in the details of any and every plan possible for doing at this late day anything like justice to the Indian, there is no difficulty in agreeing on certain things that ought not to be done. Cheating, robbing, breaking promises – these are clearly things which must cease to be done. One more thing, also, and that is the refusal of the protection of the law to the Indian's rights of property, 'of life, liberty, and the pursuit of happiness.'"xcvi

HELEN HUNT JACKSON,

ON BEHALF OF NATIVE-AMERICANS, 1881

Why do we have this limited protection of political and social speech and assembly? We have it to create a way for all views on political and social issues to be vented in a way that diffuses violence instead of creating an underground threat of it. People are heard and their opposites are heard. The public then makes up its mind, usually slowly, about proper public policy. The national Constitution protects all ideational viewpoints from government interference. It does not protect the free-speech and assembly rights of private actors, only public tax-supported ones.

In some other countries those in authority decide what is "hateful" or "appropriate" and what is not and the citizens of those countries do not have the privilege of hearing or knowing what some of their fellow-citizens think about political and social issues. It has often created, for them, a cauldron of simmering resentment for which the outlet is often violence and anarchy.

A case in point is Europe prior to WWI. This was a civilization good enough to satisfy the deepest wants of human creatures, as Sinclair Lewis put it, in Europe at the turn of the 20th century, represented by Great Britain at her zenith. Britain possessed twenty-five per cent of the land mass of the world. At Queen Victoria's Diamond Jubilee in 1897, the parade of representatives of all her dominions took hours. They were proud to be there in their very finest representations of unique cultures,

A Diverse Culture

— a lovely picture of imperial impute.

privileged as the government would have it, of learning the art of administration unmatched by any country in the world. The horses were magnificent; the organization flawless; the Queen pleased.

The British public, except the Irish, knew they were part of something stunning. They accepted the notion of a long-standing ruling class of two-hundred great families who for centuries had taken responsibility for governance. British standards in art, in culture, in breeding and demeanor, while not what Sinclair Lewis was talking about, nevertheless were accepted by all classes of persons, and the personification of those standards in the person of the Queen, later King, was a binding element in that society.

American society has no nobility either by tradition or by Constitutional law — just the opposite.

The United States Constitution, Article I, Sections 9 and 10

No Title of Nobility shall be granted by the United States.

No state shall grant any Title of Nobility.

America has no hereditary governing class and while it was thought that one might develop from the first six presidencies, none did. The concept of responsibility to govern, to secure traditional morality, to be a model of probity and class, while certainly part of the thoughts of George Washington, John Adams, Thomas Jefferson, James Madison, James Monroe never extended further. After the Civil War it became more important to make money than to serve in government, and the best and brightest Americans avoided entry into politics. For the British upper class, it was their duty to govern.

Here we had two prosperous engines of Western Civilization, each with different social binders, each with unique ways to accomplish the *unum* in social organization, one bound by a monarchy and the other bound by bundles of law, local parades, and free political and social speech and assembly. They came together in an odd way at the turn of the 20th century. America was expanding relentlessly and had a sheer energy and compulsiveness that would have been well-served by a mature and experienced ruling class while Britain had the mature and experienced ruling class but lost all in what appears to be a compulsive mad dash to cultural suicide beginning with the Boer War and ending in the catastrophe of World War I, when the pent-up, unexpressed, frustrations of many peoples of Europe all burst forth in a lava flow of sheer hatred.

What did this experienced and refined British group think of the suppressed rumblings of class warfare begun in earnest in revolutions of 1848, of assassinations all over the world, of new empires wanting to be recognized, of the development of ferocious new Krupp weaponry, of the scientific and other discoveries that seemed to imply infinite progress, of the surety that human beings would want to use industrial might for the betterment of humankind? These notions and developments took the West and its standards of civilization relative to the "deepest wants of human creatures" into a swirling pool of death and demise. Human behavior had not seemed to have progressed, and we will never know if free and open speech and assembly would have helped prevent it. In many ways the West has never recovered from WWI.

"Just take your idea from the last bloody war [WWI], wherein a race was pitted against itself, the members of which, on both sides, fought so tenaciously that they killed off each other in frightful, staggering numbers."

MARCUS GARVEY, JAMAICAN CIVIL RIGHTS LEADER,
IN A SPEECH IN NEW YORK, 1921[xcvii]

There are many other unifiers in the American culture even though various regions in the nation were settled by different groups with very different backgrounds. German immigrants have always done very well here with our Common Law heritage and solid boundaries. Two religious groups, the Mormons and the Christian Scientists, are uniquely American and have forged strong roots. I chose the American Parade as a unifier because it seems reflective of local communion in the highly individualized American society.

The Founders' brilliance in protecting political thought and social feeling relative to government control through the 1st Amendment of the

United States Constitution is an unparalleled positive addition to governance. Perhaps these are standards no European would recognize because they are not seen as traditional art, but *statecraft* for America is an art unto itself.

Will Rogers, one of America's best-known commentators on daily life, has this to say about the value of free speech, 1925:

> *"Give 'em a Hall or a Box to stand on and say 'Sic 'em, knock everything in sight' and when they have denounced everything from Bunions to Capitalistic Bath Tubs, then they will go home, write all week on another speech for Sunday and you never have any trouble with them. It's just like an exhaust on an Automobile. No matter how high priced the Car, you have to have an exit for its bad Air, and Gasses. They have got to come out. It don't do any particular harm, unless you just stand around smelling of it all the time, but who would want to follow a Car to smell of its exhaust when you could just as well be in the Car riding?"*[xcviii]

America, with her unique culture, beckons all who live and work here to get in the Car and ride and forget standing around and listening to all the "bad Air and Gasses," though the free speech that those gasses represent is essential to the smooth running of the Car itself.

13

The Energy That Sparks Our Economic System

The Promotion of Science and the Useful Arts.

To promote the Progress of Science and useful Arts, by securing for limited Times to Authors and Inventors the exclusive Right to their respective Writings and Discoveries

THE UNITED STATES CONSTITUTION, ARTICLE 1, SECTION 8

W e are a Western nation. What we take for granted every day, how we live, what we expect from life, what we assume will exist in a material sense comes from our Western roots. Nothing illuminates this fact more than the inclusion in our Common Law heritage and present-day national Constitution Patent and later Trademark protections.

Human beings with their inquisitive and inventive minds translated into a system to improve society and all humanity, Western or otherwise. Of course there are wonderfully inquisitive and inventive minds in all civilizations and we experience the benefits of all human invention, but our daily lives are intertwined with Western development, with Western luck, with Western happenstance, and are fortunate to be inheritors of the ideas of those geniuses of the Scottish Enlightenment, in particular.

The patent system, thought to have developed before the 1st century in northern Italy, combines the self-interest that is a characteristic of human nature and is individual, with progress of the social order, which is communal or collective. The United States Constitution emphasizes the rights and duties of the person but encourages, also, in Article I, the development of the good for the whole. These concepts are not in conflict

– they are in concert with one another. Take and promote an aspect of human nature that can benefit that individual and the good for the whole will follow. This concept might seem counter-intuitive, but this is the nugget of truth that William Bradford found in 1623 and that changed the prospects of the future of the colony from barely making it to successful survival.

Every aspect of one's life in Europe and America is tied, in one way or another to this thread of Common Law, one element of the bundle of positive law that includes statutes, constitutions, and regulations. Following unrest in the Dutch Low Countries in the 14th century, Edward III granted protection to exiled Flemish textile workers in hopes of building up the textile industry in England. The Flemish possessed advanced weaving techniques the King thought helpful to his country. In 1421, the Republic of Venice (a city state) granted a three-year patent to a barge system for carrying marble. In 1449, Henry VI granted a twenty-year patent for a technique to color glass. Think of the stained-glass windows you have seen and admired. You are admiring intellectual property of the 15th century.

Without a patent system creating an intellectual property right the first and the second Industrial Revolutions (steam then steel) could not have taken place or would have taken longer to take place. Not just the invention and its specifications (as required by Queen Anne in the 18th century), but also the improvements to existing inventions that takes us to all the modern aspects of life that we enjoy. "Letters that lie open" (the seal hung from the bottom of the page so it need not be broken to view document contents), meaning public disclosure of inventions and improvements, are open to the whole world at the United States Patent and Trademark Office adding to world-wide inventions and material improvements.

The magnificent Common Law is the basic and irreplaceable jewel in the American legal system as inherited from Great Britain. This is where the great adventure from survival to agrarian to commercial to industrial to technological begins and what the United States Constitution of 1787 still protects. Keep in mind a parallel tracking of America and Britain. First, in the early 17th century we were simply trying to survive and prevent widespread famine. Outposts and tiny communities had to be protected and stable food sources found and developed. Until 1623 this was a real issue in America. Britain had a powerful navy to protect its commercial interests and its colonial holdings and to provide the raw materials for manufacture and export. Often, they sold finished goods back to its American colonies through agents called factors.

Many colonists became debtors to factors for finished goods that were to be paid for by the proceeds of tobacco, rice, or other agricultural products. When these crops failed for one reason or other debts mounted to British agents. George Washington was one of the earliest to disassociate himself from the factor system by not relying solely on the fragile tobacco plant. He studied farming closely and rotated his crops at Mount Vernon to preserve the soil and developed advanced fertilizing and other systems to stay free of the British factors. Even so he struggled financially.

In Great Britain inventions in steam, in iron foundry, in textile creation changed the nature of Western advancement. Britain led the first Industrial Revolution. Commercial lords were replaced by Industrial lords and tenant farmers and their families began to move to manufacturing centers outside the home. One of the great pieces of luck for Great Britain was that their coal and ore were relatively close to the surface and these were the fuels that powered the Empire. The problem was water flooding the mines which had to be hauled out by horses and buckets in time-consuming and often ineffective ways.

Along came the great mechanical British engineers in Thomas Savery and Thomas Newcomen to deal with this problem. Savery patented the first pump in 1699 that used a vacuum system (heating then condensing) to raise the water. Newcomen partnered with Savery and added the power of steam to this pumping system to withdraw water from the mines. The original steam engine had been invented. It was cumbersome — the cylinder with piston was over seven feet high and twenty-one inches in diameter and required huge amounts of coal to produce the steam. It took 660 gallons of water to create steam; but it worked. The year was 1712. It would be twenty more years before George Washington was even born.

And then arrives James Watt, a self-taught Scot, who, with his very practical and inventive mind, improved the original design of the steam engine so that it could generate constant motion rather that the slow process of heating, then cooling, then heating again to create the vacuum needed. Watt patented his improvement around the time of our Revolution, attached a rod to create a rotary motion rather than a rocking motion and the Industrial Revolution had the workhorse it needed to change the world. Without the legal notion of patents that included improvements as well as inventions the human impetus to continue to create and design and partner with others would not have been as compelling. This is part of our Common Law heritage from Great Britain. The Industrial Revolution began with textiles.

Before James Watt's invention, cloth in Britain was made on a handloom by a father, often with the help of son or sons, from yarn spun by wife and daughters in their home. These were long hours and long days broken only by the Sabbath and dependent upon the health and capacity of the human body. It took a long time to spin enough cotton into strong enough thread for weaving and it took at least two persons to thread the shuttle through the weft and warp to make cloth. This work was done in the winter, when agricultural efforts were on hold, and an important part of a family's earnings just to survive.

Britain was also in competition with India. In 1721, they passed Acts of Parliament to protect its home textile industry. And then the inventions came, one by one, that changed everything. The flying shuttle on wheels, patented in 1733, allowed cloth to be made faster and wider; the spinning jenny, patented in 1770, created eight spindles of thread where one had been produced before; the power loom, patented in 1785, run by steam; all of which meant that Great Britain could compete internationally with India relative to cotton textiles. What were once home-bound industries became manufacturing centers with steam providing the energy and coal providing the steam. Urban manufacturing centers were born with all the attendant social ramifications. What about the raw material? What about the cotton? After Eli Whitney, an

American, invented and patented the cotton gin in 1793 to separate cotton from its seeds, the demand for cotton from America was elevated and the planter class and slavery strained to keep up with the demand. The slave trade was not Constitutionally banned until 1808.

James Watt's improved steam engine made the development of the railroad at the turn of the 19th century and all the ramifications of railroads, possible. Eli Whitney, with the financial help of Catharine Greene, widow of Nathanael Greene, America's Revolutionary War hero, put America on the map as the source of cotton for the manufacturing machine that Britain became. America was a new nation and fully in the throes of the first Industrial Revolution after its separation from Great Britain, embracing in express terms, its commitment to invention and innovation through Article I, section 8 of the United States Constitution, and the protection that the patent gives to inventors and improvers along with potential wealth.

We come at this point to the great philosophical divide in the American adventure that separates our earliest notions, 1607-1776, from our later ones. It is our concept of the nature of human beings and the relationship that human beings have with society. The question is whether human beings are basically good or basically evil, and how that question is answered accounts for the later economic system that binds our culture and is the ultimate unifier, along with our unique four bundles of law.

The Great Divide, as I will call it, is best represented by our friends from the Scottish Enlightenment, David Hume, Francis Hutcheson and a British philosopher, Thomas Hobbes. While Scots James Watt, Joseph Black, Robert Foulis, and John McAdam were inventing and improving material things, David Hume and Francis Hutcheson were addressing the larger question for human beings, possibly after the question of the existence of God, *what are human beings innately like?*[xcix]

The answer to this question determines the extent to which any social order can deliver the most progress to the most people most of the time. Thomas Hobbes saw the human condition as totally self-centered with human beings having a natural right to anything they could gain at the expense of others. He felt human beings are innately depraved. Hobbes did not believe that the spiritual or the immortal exists. Life is short. It is a nasty and brutish struggle, and the strong person wins what little there is to win.

For David Hume, the ultimate skeptic, and a kindred spirit to Thomas Hobbes, human beings are governed by their passions not their reasonableness. Society simply imposes and enforces rules to constrain their innate nature. "Rightful" behavior evolves from habit and external controls encourage certain habits. A strong hand, a strong arm, full force must be available and operative to deal with the explicit nature of people. Remember our friend William Bradford with the Separatists on the Mayflower that created a small commune at Plymouth – his was a strong hand and this strength kept the little Christian Utopia alive for a while. Others later wandered off to find a more lenient existence only to have to be rescued from starvation by the Plymouth Colony. Experience over the centuries told Hume that the best way to deal with human nature was to strictly contain it.

It is the mid-18th century contemporary of Hume, Francis Hutcheson, Professor of Moral Philosophy at the University of Glasgow, that provides the essential link between the nature of human beings, in conjunction with economist and philosopher Adam Smith, and the development of modern capitalism. This link is *optimism, not pessimism, about human nature.* This link is the opposite of cynicism and skepticism; it is a hope, a belief, a sense of the right and the moral and the good in human beings that can be identified, and promoted, and guided toward betterment for both the individual and for the community.

What Hutcheson added was an understanding of our otherwise self-interested nature, depraved or otherwise, that included an innate sense of the moral, right from wrong, including a benevolence to others. This concept, which was transferred to American culture, connects Presbyterian sin, Puritan piousness, Mormon revelation, Catholic heaven, Christian Science mindfulness, and all other ideations of belief or non-belief in a higher power into a theory of the nature of human beings that is positive. If human beings have an innate moral sense, then good for the greater number is possible. Systems can be devised to channel this morality so that both self-interest and community interest can emerge together.

In 1630, John Winthrop felt that the Covenant with God that had directed his flock to America in hopes of creating a City on a Hill included ridding the human being of the negative excesses natural to him or her so that the perfection of a Christian person could take place. This view of human nature through a negative lens was replaced with a positive one just as the Industrial Revolution was getting its legs. Marry the positive and optimistic with the economic theory of capitalism as articulated by Adam Smith in *The Wealth of Nations* along with the natural abundance of our nation and the possible becomes the probable. Capitalism creates the capital needed for innovation and expansion by creating shares of ownership in enterprises started and continued by risk-takers. Ordinary people can own these shares and become prosperous by attaching to the risk-taker even though they themselves are neither inventive nor are risk-takers.

Capitalism is an economic system that relies on the natural self-interest of the individual person as an economic motivating force that, along with free and open markets, creates a competitive environment that makes profitable enterprises possible. In helping oneself one inadvertently helps the whole. Positivism and optimism also help to create energy and drive in people. The more energy that is created the more prosperity is created and this is certainly characteristic of American enterprise.

The chief detractor of this system was the German philosopher Karl Marx, who thought that the excess value (profit) created by workers was an exploitation of the worker that leads to inevitable class conflict. Marx was determined to destroy capitalism and replace it with Socialism and then Communism after which the state would disappear. This was an international struggle in Karl Marx's eyes and required revolution as a response to the Industrial Revolution and the social conditions that grew out of that Revolution – namely the alienation of the laboring class. Unlike the anarchists that struck European leaders in the late 19th and early 20th centuries, including the assassination of President William McKinley in America, the revolutions Marx had in mind had to be organized and hence the two movements never really merged because anarchy, by definition, rejects structure.

Although there was a growing interest in the ideas of Marx in America in the late 19th century and certainly into the 20th century and 21st century, it is the optimism of Hutcheson's philosophy, in concert with the economic system of Adam Smith, which prevailed over the negativism of Hobbes and Hume and some of the German idealists. This positive view of the nature of humanity, tied to the Protestant ethic that includes charity as well as hard work, has resulted in a unique form of capitalism in America. The system has not been without its failures and it has not developed evenly. There are human costs associated with its development.

The first stages of the Industrial Revolution in America powered by steam, the discovery of oil and gold, and all the ramifications of rapacious westward expansion, including the decimation of the buffalo, created the ripest opportunity for one of humanity's worst diseases of the heart —greed. Railroads with their vast land holdings and fixed high freight rates; Standard Oil and the other predatory Trusts; capitalism without its Protestant modifier and legal restrictions; these were the early results of positive business energy and specialized labor concepts articulated by Adam Smith.

Our bundle of positive law had not anticipated the pace of the Industrial Revolution. It took Congress and the Supreme Court a long time to create its proper regulation. The factory system created cities and centers of population that at one time had been dispersed to farms. Food at one time was grown by individual families. Now massive amounts of food had to be processed to feed large numbers of people.

These were the conditions in the beef and pork packing industry as outlined by Upton Sinclair in *The Jungle*, 1906:

> *"There was never the least attention paid to what was cut up for sausage; there would come all the way back from Europe old sausage that had been rejected, and that was moldy and white – it would be dosed with borax and glycerin, and dumped into the hoppers, and made over again for home consumption. There would be meat that had tumbled on the floor ... where the workers had spit*

uncounted billions of consumption germs. There would be meat stored in great piles in rooms ... and thousands of rats would race about on it...a man might run his hand over these piles of meat and sweep off handfuls of the dried dung of rats ... the packers would put poisoned bread out for them; they would die, and then rats, bread, and meat would go into the hoppers together. Under the system of rigid economy ... there were some jobs that it only paid to do once in a long time, and among these was the cleaning out of the waste barrels. Every spring they did it ... it would be taken up and dumped into the hoppers with the fresh meat and sent out to the public's breakfast."[c]

Immigration became an issue. Workers brought into the country to provide the labor for expansion also brought with them behaviors that alarmed communities and eventually Congress. The Chinese, for instance, had been encouraged to come to help build the railroad, but in 1881, they were excluded by Congress.

"Be it enacted by the Senate and House of Representatives of the United States of America in Congress assembled, that from ninety days after the passage of this act, and until the expiration of ten years after the passage of this act, the coming of Chinese laborers to the United States be suspended .. it shall not be lawful for any Chinese laborer to come or having so come after the expiration of ninety days, to remain within the United States."[ci]

And so, one-hundred and fifty plus years (1607-1783) of survival and the development of agrarian wealth within the framework of a certain belief in the nature of human beings, became, after the American Revolution, another one hundred plus years (1783-1900) of almost unrestricted commercial and industrial development, within the framework of a different belief in the nature of human beings, and at that point America stopped and took stock of what it had become. The Progressive Movement began to look at the social costs and the environmental costs of runaway "progress."

Jane Addams, one of the best-known social reformers distinguishes the individual philanthropist from the social reformer. While one individual's efforts may be admirable, real reform comes from the democratic process and legislative action.

> *"It is as yet most difficult for us to free ourselves from the individualistic point of view sufficiently to group events in their social relations and to judge fairly those who are endeavoring to produce a social result through all the difficulties of associated action. The philanthropist still finds his path much easier than do those who are attempting a social morality... To attempt to attain a social morality without a basis of democratic experience results in the loss of the only possible corrective and guide and ends in an exaggerated individual morality but not in social morality at all."*[cii]

What Jane Addams is telling us is that for all the Andrew Carnegie libraries and all the hospital wings and all the museums and art galleries gifted by individuals it is only through legislative action that meaningful change can take place for the betterment of the whole. This is an extremely important demarcation line in the American experience in conjunction with our nation's entry into the world of international power politics. Her efforts, along with many others, led to child labor laws, as well as compulsory education laws intended to take children out of factories, and hourly and safety laws, and all the protections for labor that we have as labor law today. This legislation is one element of our statutory law and regulatory law and a part of one of the four bundles of law that govern our social order. There is always tension in our system between creativity in entrepreneurship and regulation for the general welfare.

The United States Constitution straddles the line elucidated by Jane Addams by both freeing the individual through protection of his or her invention in Patent and Trademark and strengthening the community through the legislative process intended for the general welfare of the people.

The Energy That Sparks Our Economic System

Article I, Section 8, United States Constitution:
Congress shall have Power To provide for the general Welfare of the United States ... And To make all Laws which shall be necessary and proper for carrying into Execution the foregoing Powers vested by this Constitution in the Government of the United States, or in any Department or Officer thereof.

American capitalism, through many trials and economic roller coaster rides, is basically a system which reflects our unique history, culture, and law. It has a moral, almost religious, component that requires virtue and charity and generosity. Your business word must have personal honor behind it. American capitalism has a social contract component that requires that successful businesses provide benefits and protections for employees that are not expenses transferred to the taxpayer at large but borne as a responsibility of the business.

It also has a shared wealth component that provides a way for employees to become owners, not just workers, through shares of stock in the business or franchise opportunities where appropriate. In other words, the division of labor concept that is the heart and soul of Adam Smith's vision, that is extremely productive and efficient, is required to be tethered to the consequences and ramifications of that division so that there is a minimum of human suffering associated with it. Each owner and corporation also have a high duty to patrons who use the product or services of the business and to the country at large for providing the stable social order that makes it all work. American capitalism is an economic system but not outside the strictures of ethics and virtue.

Our American journey has not been an even journey or a fair journey for all people at all times. What it has been is a *human* journey, with lessons to be learned and progress to be made, but always within the purview of personal liberty and limited tyranny. All kinds of people from all over have added their energy and their talents to the process. All who come here promise to learn and understand our four bundles of law; to enjoy and be grateful for the prosperity that our system has created within that law; and to become informed and virtuous quintessential citizens and sovereigns.

E Pluribus Unum — from many, we are one.

Conclusion

What to make of it all. In our very scattered and roundabout way we have glanced, during our twirl on the ice, at the sincere, the smart, the reasonable, the bloodthirsty, the mean; the desperate, the pragmatic, the genius, and at the sheer movement that is the magic that is America. I can't explain it.

Simone de Beauvoir, the French novelist, says this about America in 1948:

"Americans like speed, alcohol, thriller films, and any sensational news: the demand for new things, and ever new things, is feverish since nowhere will they rest ... To like America or not to like her – these words have no sense. Here is a battlefield, and one can only follow with excitement the struggle she carries on within herself, the stakes of which are beyond measure."[ciii]

One of my premises is that we Americans are both Mortar Minders and Change Agents depending upon the subject and the issue at a moment in time. Who cannot admire the mind of Thomas Jefferson, the morality of Marian Anderson, the sincerity of William Bradford? Who does not cringe at the Trail of Tears; at the snatched child from a west-African village; at the orphan from the slums of London suddenly on a ship of cruel indifference headed to America and indentured servitude? Think of those trusting little piglets in Chicago following their brothers and sisters up the ramps to their unsuspecting deaths, squealing so pitifully, just to feed the urban masses already dying from heavy cream by the gallon.

It is true that the United States Constitution was written by some remarkably intelligent, astute, and educated people. James Wilson deserves your attention; so, does Benjamin Franklin. But just when we begin to take seriously the superior intellectual gifts from our Enlightenment forefathers, we are reminded anew of the fact that we also come, on the English side, from "levelers," and "diggers," and "ranters."

These are the common people – not the "smart" people. They wanted equality, and common land to farm, and natural living without false sexual constraints.

Yoram Hazony has another view of the Enlightenment we so treasure:

> *"Enlightenment philosophy didn't achieve a fraction of the good they claim, and it has done much harm. These [earlier British] statesmen and philosophers articulated the principles of modern Anglo-American constitutionalism centuries before the U.S. was created. They were religious, English nationalists and political conservatives. A more serious claim [to modern science] can be made by the Renaissance, the period between the 15th and 17th centuries, particularly in Italy, Holland, and England. Human reason is incapable of reaching universally unassailably correct answers to the problems of science, morality, and politics by applying the methods of mathematics. The 'science' Marx developed ... killed tens of millions in the 20th century. Enlightenment overconfidence has gone badly wrong often enough to warrant serious doubts about claims made in the name of reason."*[civ]

Perhaps Hazony is right and a more serious claim to science can be made in earlier times but America does not necessarily claim credit for pure science. She might have more of a claim to practical science; to the use of science for everyday purposes; to the smokeless stove; to Useful Endeavors that make life simpler, easier, or survivable. It wasn't "science" that Marx developed, it was an idea that permeated and continues to permeate whole cultures that experimented with its well-intentioned notions and its deadly implementation. Our system that involves time-worthy universals helps shield us from the next well-intentioned but bad idea.

It is true that the United States Constitution is certainly an Enlightenment document, and certainly attempted to elevate reason to an exalted status in our supreme positive law, *a la* Immanuel Kant and others, especially in the arena of public corruption and theocracy. We have a system that diffuses government power called federalism and we rejected a national established religion the National Cathedral in

Conclusion

Washington, DC notwithstanding. The contribution of these Enlightenment concepts of statecraft, as represented in this original and inventive splitting of sovereignty, cannot be overstated. On a practical level making plenary power local keeps the restraints on human behavior local, a much more effective tool than nationalized coercion.

Because our Constitution is the Supreme positive Law of the Land, we forget that its supremacy relates only to positive law not to *all* law. Our society is governed by more than positive law although statutes and ordinances and administrative rules and fifty state constitutions and state and colonial common law overwhelm us in sheer volume. Moral law trumps positive law and unwritten law seeps into every corner of our conscious lives. While natural law remains more theoretical and less enforceable, we see its power to create discussion every time the Supreme Court of the United States rules in such a way that life itself seems less an unalienable right than a possible whim or government mandate.

In other words, our society does not depend on the United States Constitution alone for our governance. The notion that is elevated above all, even reason, is tolerance of all views, including hateful views, that forces us into a dialogue and debate with each other resulting in a kind of courteous or begrudging consensus. It is a mix of the Mortar Minder and the Change Agent on any given issue. The tension between the two is always maintained (neither side completely wins) and it is this tension that helps keep the whole social order stable.

Thomas L. Friedman expresses this mix succinctly when he said that:

"Of all the skills and knowledge that we test young people for which is the most important? the ability to master 'two codes': computer science and the U.S. Constitution ... technology and democracy are thought of as in conflict, but are actually both essential and need to work in tandem."[cv]

In other words, our culture needs the stable and the new; it needs pure science and scientific ethics; it needs obedience and liberty; it needs stay-the-course and start-all-over again; it needs the township and the nation; it needs the Change Agent and the Mortar Minder; it needs old monuments and new ones, too; it needs reminders and lessons of the past and visions and promises for the future. It needs all of these wrapped in a type of goodwill, optimism, and energy combined with a respect and reverence for the past.

The Romans were famous two thousand years ago, and are still famous today, for the quality of their compression bridges. If you can imagine the travel way on such a bridge as a pathway for social justice, the integrity of that pathway depends upon a stable social order or the construct of the bridge itself. The social justice warrior, a type of Change Agent, wants to speed to his or her desired political end upon an unencumbered travel way and often gives little thought to what is holding the bridge up in the first place. What is holding the bridge up in the first place is what concerns the Mortar Minders. Roman bridges have arches and abutments and stones in place that support the travel way. In our society the abutment that carries the full weight of our stability is the family unit itself. The health of that unit or the strength of each family is critical to the welfare of our whole society. The arches are the philosophies that undergird the rule of law, transferring the heavy weight of our social and other issues outward along their curves, and the stones in place are the laws themselves. Roman bridges did not have mortar but if they did it would represent the shared culture that we all enjoy. To go back to Simone de Beauvoir, Americans enjoy NASCAR, bars, politics as blood sport, and new technology. I would also add that Americans love to start all over again and make it work this time!

It would seem logical that if we are all both Mortar Minders and Change Agents at any given time that there would be some appreciation of this fact within each of these circles. If I am primarily a Change Agent, I want the travel way free of debris and the bridge solid beneath me. What good would it do to race to change and have the whole thing collapse under me or find out that what I thought was "reform" turned out badly and I needed to undo? On the other hand, if my focus, generally, is on making sure that the substructure remains strong, how do I account for natural change that comes with advances in knowledge and the application of that knowledge, the desire of every new generation to make its mark, and change that amounts to positive reform? It is this appreciation for both positions that seems to be missing at this moment in time.

I asked the question in the introduction, "Can the United States Constitution hold up in modern times?" The answer is, "yes", but only

- *if* there is an understanding of the rules and philosophies that undergird our social order, including the Constitution, taught to each generation.
- *if* there is an understanding that Change must take place within these rules.
- *if* there is an understanding of *why* Change must take place within these rules.
- *if* there is an understanding and appreciation for both Change Agents and Mortar Minders as important to our social order in the right degree at the right time.

Sometimes society needs to catch its breath and absorb over decades a particularly revolutionary time. No society can handle constant revolution. Constant revolution and chaos produce deadly vibrations on the bridge, called resonance, that cannot be stopped and that assures the bridge's collapse. There are generations whose duty it is to repair the abutments and secure the keystones (The Era of Good Feeling, 1815-1825); there are generations whose duty it is to sacrifice their very lives (D-Day in WWII, 1944); there are generations whose duty it is to help us understand new ways of governance (The Founders, 1787); and there are generations who ask us to re-calibrate our notions of social justice (The Civil Rights Movement, 1965-68).

The rules we play by in America have been developed over a long period of time and have been tested over and over by human experience both profoundly angelic and profoundly wicked. What has kept us steady is our four bundles of law: *moral law* or what is right and what is wrong; *natural law* or the law that wraps around each person simply by his or her existence; *positive law* that includes constitutional, statutory, common, and administrative rules; and *unwritten law* that governs our interactions with each other that includes the courteous and the kindly.

Marcus Tullius Cicero, 54 BCE, explains natural law:

"True law is right reason, consonant with nature, spread through all people. It is constant and eternal; it summons to duty by its orders, it deters from crime by its prohibitions. Its orders or prohibitions to good people are never given in vain; but it does not move the wicked ... god ...is the author, expounder, and mover of this law; and the person who does not obey it will be in exile from himself. Insofar as he scorns his nature as a human being, by this very fact he will pay the greatest penalty, even if he escapes all other things that are generally recognized as punishments."[cvi]

We, Americans, as articulated in the Preamble to the United States Constitution, value our personal liberty first and foremost. To sustain it generation after generation, we must constrain that which works tirelessly to remove it from the playing field of life – tyranny in all its forms. Those forms we recognize as concentrated power; corruption that always flows from concentrated power; unmodified greed; inhumane treatment of people and animals; disrespect for the gifts of nature and for the many blessings of this life. We recognize that what may be legal may not be lawful. There is an ethical component in human decision and behavior in all arenas of life. Tyranny can be represented by both Change Agents and Mortar Minders – it is not exclusive to one or the other.

I said earlier that I wanted you, the reader, to love and appreciate America, warts and all. Our system is not stuck in the past. It is still young and fresh and flexible and able to be properly modified as the people see fit within the objective truths we know over time; in other words, within our four bundles of law. Our history is to be treasured, not dismantled. Only the supremely arrogant and ignorant tear down those things we learn by, and through, and with, as beloved partners on our journey towards virtue and wisdom. It is supremely unfair to see the past as wanting when our brothers and sisters could not always have foreseen what we can see and what we can see will be hopelessly limited in future times.

Abraham Lincoln, in talking about the Founders, speaks to us now:

"They were the pillars of the temple of liberty; and now, that they have crumbled away, that temple must fall, unless we, their descendants supply their places with other pillars, hewn from the

solid quarry of sober reason. Let those materials be moulded into general intelligence, sound morality, and in particular, a reverence for the Constitution and laws: and, that we improved to the last; that we remained free to the last; that we revered his name [George Washington] to the last; that during his long sleep, we permitted no hostile foot to pass over or desecrate his resting place."[cvii]

What Lincoln is telling us is that we must always be a good people; we must always be a moral people; and we must always be a dutiful people. We must ask no less of ourselves than that given by Lincoln and Washington and many others who look to us now to carry on the *magic* that is America.

Acknowledgements

I am indebted beyond measure to Bonnie Walker who spent many long hours editing and producing APPLES OF GOLD and to Cathy McNeill for her careful editing. I am also indebted to Roya McCloskey, Peter Harris, Helen Bishop, and Wanda Jackson for their interest and astute comments. Thanks, also, to Darby Hollinger, who located the photographs that brought the voices to life as real people.

I encourage every reader to support lifelong learning in your community. The many years I spent teaching United States Constitutional Law allowed me to meet and get to know brilliant and inquisitive minds with widely varying views. This book encourages you to see persons who hold different political views as equally worthy and to look for common ground. Thomas Jefferson, after a very difficult and contentious election of 1800, said in his first inaugural address, "Every difference of opinion is not a difference of principle. We are all Republicans; we are all Federalists."

Bonnie Walker, the editor and producer of this book, is quintessentially open to thinking about and considering views she personally opposes. This quality is an important part of a timeless requirement that gives context and meaning to our shared experiences and keeps alive voices from the past that speak to us now.

Part of the proceeds of this book will go to the Kynder and Jentler Foundation, Inc., a tax-exempt Foundation to help ensure upward mobility for all children. *Every child's pathway to prosperity!* To kindly donate go to friendsofkynderandjentler.org

Appendices

DECLARATION OF INDEPENDENCE (1776)

When in the Course of human events it becomes necessary for one people to dissolve the political bands which have connected them with another and to assume among the powers of the earth, the separate and equal station to which the Laws of Nature and of Nature's God entitle them, a decent respect to the opinions of mankind requires that they should declare the causes which impel them to the separation.

We hold these truths to be self-evident, that all men are created equal, that they are endowed by their Creator with certain unalienable Rights, that among these are Life, Liberty and the pursuit of Happiness. — That to secure these rights, Governments are instituted among Men, deriving their just powers from the consent of the governed, — That whenever any Form of Government becomes destructive of these ends, it is the Right of the People to alter or to abolish it, and to institute new Government, laying its foundation on such principles and organizing its powers in such form, as to them shall seem most likely to affect their Safety and Happiness. Prudence, indeed, will dictate that Governments long established should not be changed for light and transient causes; and accordingly all experience hath shown that mankind are more disposed to suffer, while evils are sufferable than to right themselves by abolishing the forms to which they are accustomed. But when a long train of abuses and usurpations, pursuing invariably the same Object evinces a design to reduce them under absolute Despotism, it is their right, it is their duty, to throw off such Government, and to provide new Guards for their future security. — Such has been the patient sufferance of these Colonies; and such is now the necessity which constrains them to alter their former Systems of Government. The history of the present King of Great Britain is a history of repeated injuries and usurpations, all having in direct object the establishment of an absolute Tyranny over these States. To prove this, let Facts be submitted to a candid world.

He has refused his Assent to Laws, the most wholesome and necessary for the public good.

He has forbidden his Governors to pass Laws of immediate and pressing importance, unless suspended in their operation till his Assent should be obtained; and when so suspended, he has utterly neglected to attend to them.

He has refused to pass other Laws for the accommodation of large districts of people, unless those people would relinquish the right of Representation in the Legislature, a right inestimable to them and formidable to tyrants only.

He has called together legislative bodies at places unusual, uncomfortable, and distant from the depository of their Public Records, for the sole purpose of fatiguing them into compliance with his measures.

He has dissolved Representative Houses repeatedly, for opposing with manly firmness his invasions on the rights of the people.

He has refused for a long time, after such dissolutions, to cause others to be elected, whereby the Legislative Powers, incapable of Annihilation, have returned to the People at large for their exercise; the State remaining in the meantime exposed to all the dangers of invasion from without, and convulsions within.

He has endeavored to prevent the population of these States; for that purpose, obstructing the Laws for Naturalization of Foreigners; refusing to pass others to encourage their migrations hither, and raising the conditions of new Appropriations of Lands.

He has obstructed the Administration of Justice by refusing his Assent to Laws for establishing Judiciary Powers.

He has made Judges dependent on his Will alone for the tenure of their offices, and the amount and payment of their salaries.

He has erected a multitude of New Offices and sent hither swarms of Officers to harass our people and eat out their substance.

He has kept among us, in times of peace, Standing Armies without the Consent of our legislatures. He has affected to render the Military independent of and superior to the Civil Power.

He has combined with others to subject us to a jurisdiction foreign to our constitution, and unacknowledged by our laws, giving his Assent to their Acts of pretended Legislation:

For quartering large bodies of armed troops among us:

For protecting them, by a mock Trial from punishment for any Murders which they should commit on the Inhabitants of these States:

For cutting off our Trade with all parts of the world: For imposing Taxes on us without our Consent:

For depriving us in many cases, of the benefit of Trial by Jury:

For transporting us beyond Seas to be tried for pretended offences:

For abolishing the free System of English Laws in a neighboring Province, establishing therein an Arbitrary government, and enlarging its Boundaries so as to render it at once an example and fit instrument for introducing the same absolute rule into these Colonies

For taking away our Charters, abolishing our most valuable Laws and altering fundamentally the Forms of our Governments:

For suspending our own Legislatures and declaring themselves invested with power to legislate for us in all cases whatsoever.

He has abdicated Government here, by declaring us out of his Protection and waging War against us. He has plundered our seas, ravaged our coasts, burnt our towns, and destroyed the lives of our people.

He is at this time transporting large Armies of foreign Mercenaries to complete the works of death, desolation, and tyranny, already begun with circumstances of Cruelty & Perfidy scarcely paralleled in the most barbarous ages, and totally unworthy the Head of a civilized nation.

He has constrained our fellow Citizens taken Captive on the high Seas to bear Arms against their Country, to become the executioners of their friends and Brethren, or to fall themselves by their Hands.

He has excited domestic insurrections amongst us and has endeavored to bring on the inhabitants of our frontiers, the merciless Indian Savages whose known rule of warfare, is an undistinguished destruction of all ages, sexes and conditions.

In every stage of these Oppressions We have Petitioned for Redress in the most humble terms: Our repeated Petitions have been answered only by repeated injury. A Prince, whose character is thus marked by every act which may define a Tyrant, is unfit to be the ruler of a free people.

Nor have We been wanting in attentions to our British brethren. We have warned them from time to time of attempts by their legislature to extend an unwarrantable jurisdiction over us. We have reminded them of the circumstances of our emigration and settlement here. We have appealed to their native justice and magnanimity, and we have conjured them by the ties of our common kindred to disavow these usurpations, which would inevitably interrupt our connections and correspondence. They too have been deaf to the voice of justice and of consanguinity. We must, therefore, acquiesce in the necessity, which denounces our Separation, and hold them, as we hold the rest of mankind, Enemies in War, in Peace Friends.

We, therefore, the Representatives of the united States of America, in General Congress, Assembled, appealing to the Supreme Judge of the world for the rectitude of our intentions, do, in the Name, and by Authority of the good People of these Colonies, solemnly publish and declare, That these united Colonies are, and of Right ought to be Free and Independent States, that they are Absolved from all Allegiance to the British Crown, and that all political connection between them and the State of Great Britain, is and ought to be totally dissolved; and that as Free and Independent States, they have full Power to levy War, conclude Peace, contract Alliances, establish Commerce, and to do all other Acts and Things which Independent States may of right do. — And for the support of this Declaration, with a firm reliance on the protection of Divine Providence, we mutually pledge to each other our Lives, our Fortunes, and our sacred Honor.

ARTICLES OF CONFEDERATION AND PERPETUAL UNION (1778)

To all to whom these Presents shall come, we the undersigned Delegates of the States affixed to our Names, send greeting.

Whereas the Delegates of the United States of America, in Congress assembled, did, on the 15th day of November, in the Year of Our Lord One thousand Seven Hundred and Seventy seven, and in the Second Year of the Independence of America, agree to certain articles of Confederation and perpetual Union between the States of New-Hampshire, Massachusetts-bay, Rhode-island and Providence Plantations, Connecticut, New York, New Jersey, Pennsylvania, Delaware, Maryland, Virginia, North-Carolina, South-Carolina, and Georgia in the words following, viz. "Articles of Confederation and perpetual Union between the states of New-Hampshire, Massachusetts-bay, Rhode-island and Providence Plantations, Connecticut, New-York, New-Jersey, Pennsylvania, Delaware, Maryland, Virginia, North-Carolina, South-Carolina and Georgia."

Article I

The Stile of this confederacy shall be "The United States of America."

Article II

Each state retains its sovereignty, freedom, and independence, and every Power, Jurisdiction and right, which is not by this confederation expressly delegated to the United States, in Congress assembled.

Article III

The said states hereby severally enter into a firm league of friendship with each other, for their common defense, the security of their Liberties, and their mutual and general welfare, binding themselves to assist each other, against all force offered to, or attacks made upon them, or any of them, on account of religion, sovereignty, trade, or any other pretense whatever.

Article IV

The better to secure and perpetuate mutual friendship and intercourse among the people of the different states in this union, the free inhabitants of each of these states, paupers, vagabonds and fugitives from justice excepted, shall be entitled to all privileges and immunities of free citizens in the several states; and the people of each state shall have free ingress and regress to and from any other state, and shall enjoy therein all the privileges of trade and commerce, subject to the same duties impositions and restrictions as the inhabitants thereof respectively, provided that such restriction shall not extend so far as to prevent the removal of property imported into any state, to any other state, of which the Owner is an inhabitant; provided also that no imposition, duties or restriction shall be laid by any state, on the property of the united states, or either of them. If any Person guilty of, or charged with treason, felony, — or other high misdemeanor in any state, shall flee from Justice, and be found in any of the united states, he shall, upon demand of the Governor or executive power, of the state from which he fled, be delivered up and removed to the state having jurisdiction of his offence. Full faith and credit shall be given in each of these states to the records, acts and judicial proceedings of the courts and magistrates of every other state.

Article V

For the more convenient management of the general interests of the united states, delegates shall be annually appointed in such manner as the legislature of each state shall direct, to meet in Congress on the first Monday in November, in every year, with a power reserved to each state, to recall its delegates, or any of them, at any time within the year, and to send others in their stead, for the remainder of the Year.

No state shall be represented in Congress by less than two, nor by more than seven Members; and no person shall be capable of being a delegate for more than three years in any term of six years; nor shall any person, being a delegate, be capable of holding any office under the united states, for which he, or another for his benefit receives any salary, fees or emolument of any kind.

Each state shall maintain its own delegates in a meeting of the states, and while they act as members of the committee of the states. In determining questions in the united states in Congress assembled, each state shall have one vote.

Freedom of speech and debate in Congress shall not be impeached or questioned in any Court, or place out of Congress, and the members of congress shall be protected in their persons from arrests and imprisonments, during the time of their going to and from, and attendance on congress, except for treason, felony, or breach of the peace.

Article VI

No state, without the Consent of the united states in congress assembled, shall send any embassy to, or receive any embassy from, or enter into any conference agreement, alliance or treaty with any King prince or state; nor shall any person holding any office of profit or trust under the united states, or any of them, accept of any present, emolument, office or title of any kind whatever from any king, prince or foreign state; nor shall the united states in congress assembled, or any of them, grant any title of nobility.

No two or more states shall enter into any treaty, confederation or alliance whatever between them, without the consent of the united states in congress assembled, specifying accurately the purposes for which the same is to be entered into, and how long it shall continue.

No state shall lay any imposts or duties, which may interfere with any stipulations in treaties, entered into by the united states in congress assembled, with any king, prince or state, in pursuance of any treaties already proposed by congress, to the courts of France and Spain.

No vessels of war shall be kept up in time of peace by any state, except such number only, as shall be deemed necessary by the united states in congress assembled, for the defense of such state, or its trade; nor shall anybody of forces be kept up by any state, in time of peace, except such number only, as in the judgment of the united states, in congress assembled, shall be deemed requisite to garrison the forts necessary for the defense of such state; but every state shall always keep up a well-regulated and disciplined militia, sufficiently armed and accoutered, and shall provide and constantly have ready for use, in public stores, a due number of field pieces and tents, and a proper quantity of arms, ammunition and camp equipage. No state shall engage in any war without the consent of the united states in congress assembled, unless such state be actually invaded by enemies, or shall have received certain advice of a resolution being formed by some nation of Indians to invade such state, and the danger is so imminent as not to admit of a delay till the united states in congress assembled can be consulted: nor shall any state grant commissions to any ships or vessels of war, nor letters of marque or reprisal, except it be after a declaration of war by the united states in congress assembled, and then only against the kingdom or state and the subjects thereof, against which war has been so declared, and under such regulations as shall be established by the united states in congress assembled, unless such state be infested by pirates, in which case vessels of war may be fitted out for that occasion, and kept so long as the danger shall continue, or until the united states in congress assembled, shall determine otherwise.

Article VII

When land-forces are raised by any state for the common defense, all officers of or under the rank of colonel, shall be appointed by the legislature of each state respectively, by whom such forces shall be raised, or in such manner as such state shall direct, and all vacancies shall be filled up by the State which first made the appointment.

Article VIII

All charges of war, and all other expenses that shall be incurred for the common defense or general welfare, and allowed by the united states in congress assembled, shall be def rayed out of a common treasury, which shall be supplied by the several states in proportion to the value of all land within each state, granted to or surveyed for any Person, as such land and the buildings and improvements thereon shall be estimated according to such mode as the united states in congress assembled, shall from time to time direct and appoint.

The taxes for paying that proportion shall be laid and levied by the authority and direction of the legislatures of the several states within the time agreed upon by the united states in congress assembled.

Article IX

The united states in congress assembled, shall have the sole and exclusive right and power of determining on peace and war, except in the cases mentioned in the sixth article — of sending and receiving ambassadors — entering into treaties and alliances, provided that no treaty of commerce shall be made whereby the legislative power of the respective states shall be restrained from imposing such imposts and duties on foreigners as their own people are subjected to, or from prohibiting the exportation or importation of any species of goods or commodities, whatsoever — of establishing rules for deciding in all cases, what captures on land or water shall be legal, and in what manner prizes taken by land or naval forces in the service of the united states shall be divided or appropriated — of granting letters of marque and reprisal in times of peace — appointing courts for the trial of piracies and felonies committed on the high seas and establishing courts for receiving and determining finally appeals in all cases of captures, provided that no member of congress shall be appointed a judge of any of the said courts.

The united states in congress assembled shall also be the last resort on appeal in all disputes and differences now subsisting or that hereafter may arise between two or more states concerning boundary, jurisdiction or any other cause whatever; which authority shall always be exercised in the manner following. Whenever the legislative or executive authority or lawful agent of any state in controversy with another shall present a petition to congress stating the matter in question and praying for a hearing, notice thereof shall be given by order of congress to the legislative or executive authority of the other state in controversy, and a day assigned for the appearance of the parties by their lawful agents, who shall then be directed to appoint by joint consent, commissioners or judges to constitute a court for hearing and determining the matter in question: but if they cannot agree, congress shall name three persons out of each of the united states, and from the list of such persons each party shall alternately strike out one, the petitioners beginning, until the number shall be reduced to thirteen; and from that number not less than seven, nor more than nine names as congress shall direct, shall in the presence of congress be drawn out by lot, and the persons whose names shall be so drawn or any five of them, shall be commissioners or judges, to hear and finally determine the controversy, so always as a major part of the judges who shall hear the cause shall agree in the determination: and if either party shall neglect to attend at the day appointed, without showing reasons, which congress shall judge sufficient, or being present shall refuse to strike, the congress shall proceed to nominate three persons out of each state, and the secretary of congress shall strike in behalf of such party absent or refusing; and the judgment and sentence of the court to be appointed, in the manner before prescribed, shall be final and conclusive; and if any of the parties shall refuse to submit to the authority of such court, or to appear or defend their claim or cause, the court shall nevertheless proceed to pronounce sentence, or judgment, which shall in like manner be final and decisive, the judgment or sentence and other proceedings being in either case transmitted to congress, and lodged among the acts of congress for the security of the parties concerned: provided that every commissioner, before he sits in judgment, shall take an oath to be administered by one of the judges of the supreme or superior court of the state, where the cause shall be tried, well and truly to hear and determine the matter in question, according to the best of his judgment, without favour, affection or hope of reward: provided also, that no state shall be deprived of territory for the benefit of the united states.

All controversies concerning the private right of soil claimed under different grants of two or more states, whose jurisdictions as they may respect such lands, and the states which passed such grants are adjusted, the said grants or either of them being at the same time claimed to have originated antecedent to such settlement of jurisdiction, shall on the petition of either party to the congress of the united states, be finally determined as near as may be in the same manner as is before prescribed for deciding disputes respecting territorial jurisdiction between different states.

The united states in congress assembled shall also have the sole and exclusive right and power of regulating the alloy and value of coin struck by their own authority, or by that of the respective states — fixing the standard of weights and measures throughout the united states — regulating the trade and managing all affairs with the Indians, not members of any of the states, provided that the legislative right of any state within its own limits be not infringed or violated — establishing or regulating post offices from one state to another, throughout all the united states, and exacting such postage on the papers passing through' the same as may be requisite to defray the expenses of the said office — appointing all officers of the land forces, in the service of the united states, excepting regimental officers — appointing all the officers of the naval forces, and commissioning all officers whatever in the service of the united states — making rules for the government and regulation of the said land and naval forces, and directing their operations.

The united states in congress assembled shall have authority to appoint a committee, to sit in the recess of congress, to be denominated "A Committee of the States," and to consist of one delegate from each state; and to appoint such other committees and civil officers as may be necessary for managing the general affairs of the united states under their direction — to appoint one of their number to preside, provided that no person be allowed to serve in the office of president more than one year in any term of three years; to ascertain the necessary sums of money to be raised for the service of the united states, and to appropriate and apply the same for defraying the public expenses to borrow money, or emit bills on the credit of the united states, transmitting every half year to the respective states an account of the sums of money so borrowed or emitted, — to build and equip a navy — to agree upon the number of land forces, and to make requisitions from each state for its quota, in proportion to the number of white inhabitants in such state; which requisition shall be binding, and thereupon the legislature of each state shall appoint the regimental officers, raise the men and cloth, arm and equip them in a soldier like manner, at the expense of the united states; and the officers and men so clothed, armed and quipped shall march to the place appointed, and within the time agreed on by the united states in congress assembled: But if the united states in congress assembled shall, on consideration of circumstances judge proper that any state should not raise men, or should raise a smaller number than its quota, and that any other state should raise a greater number of men than the quota thereof, such extra number shall be raised, officered, clothed, armed and equipped in the same manner as the quota of such state, unless the legislature of such state shall judge that such extra number cannot be safely spared out of the same, in which case they shall raise officer, clothe, arm and equip as many of such extra number as they judge can be safely spared. And the officers and men so clothed, armed and equipped, shall march to the place appointed, and within the time agreed on by the united states in congress assembled.

The united states in congress assembled shall never engage in a war, nor grant letters of marque and reprisal in time of peace, nor enter into any treaties or alliances, nor coin money, nor regulate the value thereof, nor ascertain the sums and expenses necessary for the defense and welfare of the united states, or any of them, nor emit bills, nor borrow money on the credit of the united states, nor appropriate money, nor agree upon the number of vessels of war, to be built or purchased, or the number of land or sea forces to be raised, nor appoint a commander in chief of the army or navy, unless nine states assent to the same: nor shall a question on any other point, except for adjourning from day to day be determined, unless by the votes of a majority of the united states in congress assembled.

The congress of the united states shall have power to adjourn to any time within the year, and to any place within the united states, so that no period of adjournment be for a longer duration than the space of six Months, and shall publish the Journal of their proceedings monthly, except such parts thereof relating to treaties, alliances or military operations, as in their judgment require secrecy; and the yeas and nays of the delegates of each state on any question shall be entered on the Journal, when it is desired by any delegate; and the delegates of a state, or any of them, at his or their request shall be furnished with a transcript of the said Journal, except such parts as are above excepted, to lay before the legislatures of the several states.

Article X

The committee of the states, or any nine of them, shall be authorized to execute, in the recess of congress, such of the powers of congress as the united states in congress assembled, by the consent of nine states, shall from time to time think expedient to vest them with; provided that no power be delegated to the said committee, for the exercise of which, by the articles of confederation, the voice of nine states in the congress of the united states assembled is requisite.

Article XI

Canada acceding to this confederation, and joining in the measures of the united states, shall be admitted into, and entitled to all the advantages of this union: but no other colony shall be admitted into the same, unless such admission be agreed to by nine states.

Article XII

All bills of credit emitted, monies borrowed and debts contracted by, or under the authority of congress, before the assembling of the united states, in pursuance of the present confederation, shall be deemed and considered as a charge against the united states, for payment and satisfaction whereof the said united states, and the public faith are hereby solemnly pledged.

Article XIII

Every state shall abide by the determinations of the united states in congress assembled, on all questions which by this confederation are submitted to them. And the Articles of this confederation shall be inviolably observed by every state, and the union shall be perpetual; nor shall any alteration at any time hereafter be made in any of them; unless such alteration be agreed to in a congress of the united states, and be afterwards confirmed by the legislatures of every state.

And Whereas it hath pleased the Great Governor of the World to incline the hearts of the legislatures we respectively represent in congress, to approve of, and to authorize us to ratify the said articles of confederation and perpetual union. Know Ye that we the undersigned delegates, by virtue of the power and authority to us given for that purpose, do by these presents, in the name and in behalf of our respective constituents, fully and entirely ratify and confirm each and every of the said articles of confederation and perpetual union, and all and singular the matters and things therein contained: And we do further solemnly plight and engage the faith of our respective constituents, that they shall abide by the determinations of the united states in congress assembled, on all questions, which by the said confederation are submitted to them. And that the articles thereof shall be inviolably observed by the states we respectively represent, and that the union shall be perpetual.

In Witness whereof we have hereunto set our hands in Congress. Done at Philadelphia in the state of Pennsylvania the ninth day of July in the Year of our Lord one Thousand seven Hundred and Seventy-eight, and in the third year of the independence of America.

NORTHWEST ORDINANCE (1787)

An Ordinance for the government of the Territory of the United States northwest of the River Ohio.

Section 1

Be it ordained by the United States in Congress assembled, That the said territory, for the purposes of temporary government, be one district, subject, however, to be divided into two districts, as future circumstances may, in the opinion of Congress, make it expedient.

Section 2

Be it ordained by the authority aforesaid, That the estates, both of resident and nonresident proprietors in the said territory, dying intestate, shall descent to, and be distributed among their children, and the descendants of a deceased child, in equal parts; the descendants of a deceased child or grandchild to take the share of their deceased parent in equal parts among them: And where there shall be no children or descendants, then in equal parts to the next of kin in equal degree; and among collaterals, the children of a deceased brother or sister of the intestate shall have, in equal parts among them, their deceased parents' share; and there shall in no case be a distinction between kindred of the whole and half-blood; saving, in all cases, to the widow of the intestate her third part of the real estate for life, and one third part of the personal estate; and this law relative to descents and dower, shall remain in full force until altered by the legislature of the district. And until the governor and judges shall adopt laws as hereinafter mentioned, estates in the said territory may be devised or bequeathed by wills in writing, signed and sealed by him or her in whom the estate may be (being of full age), and attested by three witnesses; and real estates may be conveyed by lease and release, or bargain and sale, signed, sealed and delivered by the person being of full age, in whom the estate may be, and attested by two witnesses, provided such wills be duly proved, and such conveyances be acknowledged, or the execution thereof duly proved, and be recorded within one year after proper magistrates, courts, and registers shall be appointed for that purpose; and personal property may be transferred by delivery; saving, however to the French and Canadian inhabitants, and other settlers of the Kaskaskies, St. Vincents and the neighboring villages who have heretofore professed themselves citizens of Virginia, their laws and customs now in force among them, relative to the descent and conveyance, of property.

Section 3

Be it ordained by the authority aforesaid, That there shall be appointed from time to time by Congress, a governor, whose commission shall continue in force for the term of three years, unless sooner revoked by Congress; he shall reside in the district, and have a freehold estate therein in 1,000 acres of land, while in the exercise of his office.

Section 4

There shall be appointed from time to time by Congress, a secretary, whose commission shall continue in force for four years unless sooner revoked; he shall reside in the district, and have a freehold estate therein in 500 acres of land, while in the exercise of his office. It shall be his duty to keep and preserve the acts and laws passed by the legislature, and the public records of the district, and the proceedings of the governor in his executive department, and transmit authentic copies of such acts and proceedings, every six months, to the Secretary of Congress: There shall also be appointed a court to consist of three judges, any two of whom to form a court, who shall have a common law jurisdiction, and reside in the district, and have each therein a freehold estate in 500 acres of land while in the exercise of their offices; and their commissions shall continue in force during good behavior.

Section 5

The governor and judges, or a majority of them, shall adopt and publish in the district such laws of the original States, criminal and civil, as may be necessary and best suited to the circumstances of the district, and report them to Congress from time to time: which laws shall be in force in the district until the organization of the General Assembly therein, unless disapproved of by Congress; but afterwards the Legislature shall have authority to alter them as they shall think fit.

Section 6

The governor, for the time being, shall be commander in chief of the militia, appoint and commission all officers in the same below the rank of general officers; all general officers shall be appointed and commissioned by Congress.

Section 7

Previous to the organization of the general assembly, the governor shall appoint such magistrates and other civil officers in each county or township, as he shall find necessary for the preservation of the peace and good order in the same: After the general assembly shall be organized, the powers and duties of the magistrates and other civil officers shall be regulated and defined by the said assembly; but all magistrates and other civil officers not herein otherwise directed, shall during the continuance of this temporary government, be appointed by the governor.

Section 8

For the prevention of crimes and injuries, the laws to be adopted or made shall have force in all parts of the district, and for the execution of process, criminal and civil, the governor shall make proper divisions thereof; and he shall proceed from time to time as circumstances may require, to lay out the parts of the district in which the Indian titles shall have been extinguished, into counties and townships, subject, however, to such alterations as may thereafter be made by the legislature.

Section 9

So soon as there shall be five thousand free male inhabitants of full age in the district, upon giving proof thereof to the governor, they shall receive authority, with time and place, to elect a representative from their counties or townships to represent them in the general assembly: Provided, That, for every five hundred free male inhabitants, there shall be one representative, and so on progressively with the number of free male inhabitants shall the right of representation increase, until the number of representatives shall amount to twenty five; after which, the number and proportion of representatives shall be regulated by the legislature: Provided, That no person be eligible or qualified to act as a representative unless he shall have been a citizen of one of the United States three years, and be a resident in the district, or unless he shall have resided in the district three years; and, in either case, shall likewise hold in his own right, in fee simple, two hundred acres of land within the same; Provided, also, That a freehold in fifty acres of land in the district, having been a citizen of one of the states, and being resident in the district, or the like freehold and two years residence in the district, shall be necessary to qualify a man as an elector of a representative.

Section 10

The representatives thus elected, shall serve for the term of two years; and, in case of the death of a representative, or removal from office, the governor shall issue a writ to the county or township for which he was a member, to elect another in his stead, to serve for the residue of the term.

Section 11

The general assembly or legislature shall consist of the governor, legislative council, and a house of representatives. The Legislative Council shall consist of five members, to continue in office five years, unless sooner removed by Congress; any three of whom to be a quorum: and the members of the Council shall be nominated and appointed in the following manner, to wit: As soon as representatives shall be elected, the Governor shall appoint a time and place for them to meet together; and, when met, they shall nominate ten persons, residents in the district, and each possessed of a freehold in five hundred acres of land, and return their names to Congress; five of whom Congress shall appoint and commission to serve as aforesaid; and, whenever a vacancy shall happen in the council, by death or removal from office, the house of representatives shall nominate two persons, qualified as aforesaid, for each vacancy, and return their names to Congress; one of whom congress shall appoint and commission for the residue of the term. And every five years, four months at least before the expiration of the time of service of the members of council, the said house shall nominate ten persons, qualified as aforesaid, and return their names to Congress; five of whom Congress shall appoint and commission to serve as members of the council five years, unless sooner removed. And the governor, legislative council, and house of representatives, shall have authority to make laws in all cases, for the good government of the district, not repugnant to the principles and articles in this ordinance established and declared. And all bills, having passed by a majority in the house, and by a majority in the council, shall be referred to the governor for his assent; but no bill, or legislative act whatever, shall be of any force without his assent. The governor shall have power to convene, prorogue, and dissolve the general assembly, when, in his opinion, it shall be expedient.

Section 12

The governor, judges, legislative council, secretary, and such other officers as Congress shall appoint in the district, shall take an oath or affirmation of fidelity and of office; the governor before the president of congress, and all other officers before the Governor. As soon as a legislature shall be formed in the district, the council and house assembled in one room, shall have authority, by joint ballot, to elect a delegate to Congress, who shall have a seat in Congress, with a right of debating but not voting during this temporary government.

Section 13

And, for extending the fundamental principles of civil and religious liberty, which form the basis whereon these republics, their laws and constitutions are erected; to fix and establish those principles as the basis of all laws, constitutions, and governments, which forever hereafter shall be formed in the said territory: to provide also for the establishment of States, and permanent government therein, and for their admission to a share in the federal councils on an equal footing with the original States, at as early periods as may be consistent with the general interest:

Section 14

It is hereby ordained and declared by the authority aforesaid, That the following articles shall be considered as articles of compact between the original States and the people and States in the said territory and forever remain unalterable, unless by common consent, to wit:

Article 1

No person, demeaning himself in a peaceable and orderly manner, shall ever be molested on account of his mode of worship or religious sentiments, in the said territory.

Article 2

The inhabitants of the said territory shall always be entitled to the benefits of the writ of habeas corpus, and of the trial by jury; of a proportionate representation of the people in the legislature; and of judicial proceedings according to the course of the common law. All persons shall be bailable, unless for capital offenses, where the proof shall be evident or the presumption great. All fines shall be moderate; and no cruel or unusual punishments shall be inflicted. No man shall be deprived of his liberty or property, but by the judgment of his peers or the law of the land; and, should the public exigencies make it necessary, for the common preservation, to take any person's property, or to demand his particular services, full compensation shall be made for the same. And, in the just preservation of rights and property, it is understood and declared, that no law ought ever to be made, or have force in the said territory, that shall, in any manner whatever, interfere with or affect private contracts or engagements, bona fide, and without fraud, previously formed.

Article 3

Religion, morality, and knowledge, being necessary to good government and the happiness of mankind, schools and the means of education shall forever be encouraged. The utmost good faith shall always be observed towards the Indians; their lands and property shall never be taken from them without their consent; and, in their property, rights, and liberty, they shall never be invaded or disturbed, unless in just and lawful wars authorized by Congress; but laws founded in justice and humanity, shall from time to time be made for preventing wrongs being done to them, and for preserving peace and friendship with them.

Article 4

The said territory, and the States which may be formed therein, shall forever remain a part of this Confederacy of the United States of America, subject to the Articles of Confederation, and to such alterations therein as shall be constitutionally made; and to all the acts and ordinances of the United States in Congress assembled, conformable thereto. The inhabitants and settlers in the said territory shall be subject to pay a part of the federal debts contracted or to be contracted, and a proportional part of the expenses of government, to be apportioned on them by Congress according to the same common rule and measure by which apportionments thereof shall be made on the other States; and the taxes for paying their proportion shall be laid and levied by the authority and direction of the legislatures of the district or districts, or new States, as in the original States, within the time agreed upon by the United States in Congress assembled. The legislatures of those districts or new States, shall never interfere with the primary disposal of the soil by the United States in Congress assembled, nor with any regulations Congress may find necessary for securing the title in such soil to the bona fide purchasers. No tax shall be imposed on lands the property of the United States; and, in no case, shall nonresident proprietors be taxed higher than residents. The navigable waters leading into the Mississippi and St. Lawrence, and the carrying places between the same, shall be common highways and forever free, as well to the inhabitants of the said territory as to the citizens of the United States, and those of any other States that may be admitted into the confederacy, without any tax, impost, or duty therefor.

Article 5

There shall be formed in the said territory, not less than three nor more than five States; and the boundaries of the States, as soon as Virginia shall alter her act of cession, and consent to the same, shall become fixed and established as follows, to wit: The western State in the said territory, shall be bounded by the Mississippi, the Ohio, and Wabash Rivers; a direct line drawn from the Wabash and Post Vincents, due North, to the territorial line between the United States and Canada; and, by the said territorial line, to the Lake of the Woods and Mississippi. The middle State shall be bounded by the said direct line, the Wabash from Post Vincents to the Ohio, by the Ohio, by a direct line, drawn due north from the mouth of the Great Miami, to the said territorial line, and by the said territorial line. The eastern State shall be bounded by the last mentioned direct line, the Ohio, Pennsylvania, and the said territorial line: Provided, however, and it is further understood and declared, that the boundaries of these three States shall be subject so far to be altered, that, if Congress shall hereafter find it expedient, they shall have authority to form one or two States in that part of the said territory which lies north of an east and west line drawn through the southerly bend or extreme of Lake Michigan. And, whenever any of the said States shall have sixty thousand free inhabitants therein, such State shall be admitted, by its delegates, into the Congress of the United States, on an equal footing with the original States in all respects whatever, and shall be at liberty to form a permanent constitution and State government: Provided, the constitution and government so to be formed, shall be republican, and in conformity to the principles contained in these articles; and, so far as it can be consistent with the general interest of the confederacy, such admission shall be allowed at an earlier period, and when there may be a less number of free inhabitants in the State than sixty thousand.

Article 6

There shall be neither slavery nor involuntary servitude in the said territory, otherwise than in the punishment of crimes whereof the party shall have been duly convicted: Provided, always, That any person escaping into the same, from whom labor or service is lawfully claimed in any one of the original States, such fugitive may be lawfully reclaimed and conveyed to the person claiming his or her labor or service as aforesaid.

Be it ordained by the authority aforesaid, That the resolutions of the 23rd of April 1784, relative to the subject of this ordinance, be, and the same are hereby repealed and declared null and void.

Done by the United States, in Congress assembled, the 13th day of July, in the year of our Lord 1787, and of their sovereignty and independence the twelfth.

U.S. CONSTITUTION (1787)

We the People of the United States, in Order to form a more perfect Union, establish Justice, ensure domestic Tranquility, provide for the common defence, promote the general Welfare, and secure the Blessings of Liberty to ourselves and our Posterity, do ordain and establish this Constitution for the United States of America.

Article I

Section. 1

All legislative Powers herein granted shall be vested in a Congress of the United States, which shall consist of a Senate and House of Representatives.

Section. 2

The House of Representatives shall be composed of Members chosen every second Year by the People of the several States, and the Electors in each State shall have the Qualifications requisite for Electors of the most numerous Branch of the State Legislature.

No Person shall be a Representative who shall not have attained to the Age of twenty five Years, and been seven Years a Citizen of the United States, and who shall not, when elected, be an Inhabitant of that State in which he shall be chosen.

Representatives and direct Taxes shall be apportioned among the several States which may be included within this Union, according to their respective Numbers, which shall be determined by adding to the whole Number of free Persons, including those bound to Service for a Term of Years, and excluding Indians not taxed, three fifths of all other Persons. The actual Enumeration shall be made within three Years after the first Meeting of the Congress of the United States, and within every subsequent Term of ten Years, in such Manner as they shall by Law direct. The Number of Representatives shall not exceed one for every thirty Thousand, but each State shall have at Least one Representative; and until such enumeration shall be made, the State of New Hampshire shall be entitled to chuse three, Massachusetts eight, Rhode-Island and Providence Plantations one, Connecticut five, New-York six, New

Jersey four, Pennsylvania eight, Delaware one, Maryland six, Virginia ten, North Carolina five, South Carolina five, and Georgia three.

When vacancies happen in the Representation from any State, the Executive Authority thereof shall issue Writs of Election to fill such Vacancies.

The House of Representatives shall chuse their Speaker and other Officers; and shall have the sole Power of Impeachment.

Section. 3

The Senate of the United States shall be composed of two Senators from each State, chosen by the Legislature thereof, for six Years; and each Senator shall have one Vote.

Immediately after they shall be assembled in Consequence of the first Election, they shall be divided as equally as may be into three Classes. The Seats of the Senators of the first Class shall be vacated at the Expiration of the second Year, of the second Class at the Expiration of the fourth Year, and of the third Class at the Expiration of the sixth Year, so that one third may be chosen every second Year; and if Vacancies happen by Resignation, or otherwise, during the Recess of the Legislature of any State, the Executive thereof may make temporary Appointments until the next Meeting of the Legislature, which shall then fill such Vacancies.

No Person shall be a Senator who shall not have attained to the Age of thirty Years, and been nine Years a Citizen of the United States, and who shall not, when elected, be an Inhabitant of that State for which he shall be chosen.

The Vice President of the United States shall be President of the Senate, but shall have no Vote, unless they be equally divided.

The Senate shall chuse their other Officers, and also a President pro tempore, in the Absence of the Vice President, or when he shall exercise the Office of President of the United States.

The Senate shall have the sole Power to try all Impeachments. When sitting for that Purpose, they shall be on Oath or Affirmation. When the President of the United States is tried, the Chief Justice shall preside:

And no Person shall be convicted without the Concurrence of two thirds of the Members present.

Judgment in Cases of Impeachment shall not extend further than to removal from Office, and disqualification to hold and enjoy any Office of honor, Trust or Profit under the United States: but the Party convicted shall nevertheless be liable and subject to Indictment, Trial, Judgment and Punishment, according to Law.

Section. 4

The Times, Places and Manner of holding Elections for Senators and Representatives, shall be prescribed in each State by the Legislature thereof; but the Congress may at any time by Law make or alter such Regulations, except as to the Places of chusing Senators.

The Congress shall assemble at least once in every Year, and such Meeting shall be on the first Monday in December, unless they shall by Law appoint a different Day.

Section. 5

Each House shall be the Judge of the Elections, Returns and Qualifications of its own Members, and a Majority of each shall constitute a Quorum to do Business; but a smaller Number may adjourn from day to day, and may be authorized to compel the Attendance of absent Members, in such Manner, and under such Penalties as each House may provide.

Each House may determine the Rules of its Proceedings, punish its Members for disorderly Behaviour, and, with the Concurrence of two thirds, expel a Member.

Each House shall keep a Journal of its Proceedings, and from time to time publish the same, excepting such Parts as may in their Judgment require Secrecy; and the Yeas and Nays of the Members of either House on any question shall, at the Desire of one fifth of those Present, be entered on the Journal.

Neither House, during the Session of Congress, shall, without the Consent of the other, adjourn for more than three days, nor to any other Place than that in which the two Houses shall be sitting.

Section. 6

The Senators and Representatives shall receive a Compensation for their Services, to be ascertained by Law, and paid out of the Treasury of the United States. They shall in all Cases, except Treason, Felony and Breach of the Peace, be privileged from Arrest during their Attendance at the Session of their respective Houses, and in going to and returning from the same; and for any Speech or Debate in either House, they shall not be questioned in any other Place.

No Senator or Representative shall, during the Time for which he was elected, be appointed to any civil Office under the Authority of the United States, which shall have been created, or the Emoluments whereof shall have been increased during such time; and no Person holding any Office under the United States, shall be a Member of either House during his Continuance in Office.

Section. 7

All Bills for raising Revenue shall originate in the House of Representatives; but the Senate may propose or concur with Amendments as on other Bills.

Every Bill which shall have passed the House of Representatives and the Senate, shall, before it become a Law, be presented to the President of the United States; If he approve he shall sign it, but if not he shall return it, with his Objections to that House in which it shall have originated, who shall enter the Objections at large on their Journal, and proceed to reconsider it. If after such Reconsideration two thirds of that House shall agree to pass the Bill, it shall be sent, together with the Objections, to the other House, by which it shall likewise be reconsidered, and if approved by two thirds of that House, it shall become a Law. But in all such Cases the Votes of both Houses shall be determined by yeas and Nays, and the Names of the Persons voting for and against the Bill shall be entered on the Journal of each House respectively. If any Bill shall not be returned by the President within ten Days (Sundays excepted) after it shall have been presented to him, the Same shall be a Law, in like Manner as if he had signed it, unless the Congress by their Adjournment prevent its Return, in which Case it shall not be a Law.

Every Order, Resolution, or Vote to which the Concurrence of the Senate and House of Representatives may be necessary (except on a question of Adjournment) shall be presented to the President of the United States; and before the Same shall take Effect, shall be approved by him, or being disapproved by him, shall be repassed by two thirds of the Senate and House of Representatives, according to the Rules and Limitations prescribed in the Case of a Bill.

Section. 8

The Congress shall have Power To lay and collect Taxes, Duties, Imposts and Excises, to pay the Debts and provide for the common Defence and general Welfare of the United States; but all Duties, Imposts and Excises shall be uniform throughout the United States;

To borrow Money on the credit of the United States.

To regulate Commerce with foreign Nations, and among the several States, and with the Indian Tribes.

To establish a uniform Rule of Naturalization, and uniform Laws on the subject of Bankruptcies throughout the United States.

To coin Money, regulate the Value thereof, and of foreign Coin, and fix the Standard of Weights and Measures.

To provide for the Punishment of counterfeiting the Securities and current Coin of the United States.

To establish Post Offices and post Roads.

To promote the Progress of Science and useful Arts, by securing for limited Times to Authors and Inventors the exclusive Right to their respective Writings and Discoveries.

To constitute Tribunals inferior to the supreme Court.

To define and punish Piracies and Felonies committed on the high Seas, and Offences against the Law of Nations.

To declare War, grant Letters of Marque and Reprisal, and make Rules concerning Captures on Land and Water.

To raise and support Armies, but no Appropriation of Money to that Use shall be for a longer Term than two Years.

To provide and maintain a Navy.

To make Rules for the Government and Regulation of the land and naval Forces.

To provide for calling forth the Militia to execute the Laws of the Union, suppress Insurrections and repel Invasions.

To provide for organizing, arming, and disciplining, the Militia, and for governing such Part of them as may be employed in the Service of the United States, reserving to the States respectively, the Appointment of the Officers, and the Authority of training the Militia according to the discipline prescribed by Congress;

To exercise exclusive Legislation in all Cases whatsoever, over such District (not exceeding ten Miles square) as may, by Cession of particular States, and the Acceptance of Congress, become the Seat of the Government of the United States, and to exercise like Authority over all Places purchased by the Consent of the Legislature of the State in which the Same shall be, for the Erection of Forts, Magazines, Arsenals, dock-Yards, and other needful Buildings;—And

To make all Laws which shall be necessary and proper for carrying into Execution the foregoing Powers, and all other Powers vested by this Constitution in the Government of the United States, or in any Department or Officer thereof.

Section. 9

The Migration or Importation of such Persons as any of the States now existing shall think proper to admit, shall not be prohibited by the Congress prior to the Year one thousand eight hundred and eight, but a Tax or duty may be imposed on such Importation, not exceeding ten dollars for each Person.

The Privilege of the Writ of Habeas Corpus shall not be suspended, unless when in Cases of Rebellion or Invasion the public Safety may require it.

No Bill of Attainder or ex post facto Law shall be passed.

No Capitation, or other direct, Tax shall be laid, unless in Proportion to the Census or enumeration herein before directed to be taken.

No Tax or Duty shall be laid on Articles exported from any State.

No Preference shall be given by any Regulation of Commerce or Revenue to the Ports of one State over those of another: nor shall Vessels bound to, or from, one State, be obliged to enter, clear, or pay Duties in another.

No Money shall be drawn from the Treasury, but in Consequence of Appropriations made by Law; and a regular Statement and Account of the Receipts and Expenditures of all public Money shall be published from time to time.

No Title of Nobility shall be granted by the United States: And no Person holding any Office of Profit or Trust under them, shall, without the Consent of the Congress, accept of any present, Emolument, Office, or Title, of any kind whatever, from any King, Prince, or foreign State.

Section. 10

No State shall enter into any Treaty, Alliance, or Confederation; grant Letters of Marque and Reprisal; coin Money; emit Bills of Credit; make any Thing but gold and silver Coin a Tender in Payment of Debts; pass any Bill of Attainder, ex post facto Law, or Law impairing the Obligation of Contracts, or grant any Title of Nobility.

No State shall, without the Consent of the Congress, lay any Imposts or Duties on Imports or Exports, except what may be absolutely necessary for executing it's inspection Laws: and the net Produce of all Duties and Imposts, laid by any State on Imports or Exports, shall be for the Use of the Treasury of the United States; and all such Laws shall be subject to the Revision and Control of the Congress.

No State shall, without the Consent of Congress, lay any Duty of Tonnage, keep Troops, or Ships of War in time of Peace, enter into any Agreement or Compact with another State, or with a foreign Power, or engage in War, unless actually invaded, or in such imminent Danger as will not admit of delay.

Article II

Section. 1

The executive Power shall be vested in a President of the United States of America. He shall hold his Office during the Term of four Years, and, together with the Vice President, chosen for the same Term, be elected, as follows

Each State shall appoint, in such Manner as the Legislature thereof may direct, a Number of Electors, equal to the whole Number of Senators and Representatives to which the State may be entitled in the Congress: but no Senator or Representative, or Person holding an Office of Trust or Profit under the United States, shall be appointed an Elector.

The Electors shall meet in their respective States, and vote by Ballot for two Persons, of whom one at least shall not be an Inhabitant of the same State with themselves. And they shall make a List of all the Persons voted for, and of the Number of Votes for each; which List they shall sign and certify, and transmit sealed to the Seat of the Government of the United States, directed to the President of the Senate. The President of the Senate shall, in the Presence of the Senate and House of Representatives, open all the Certificates, and the Votes shall then be counted. The Person having the greatest Number of Votes shall be the President, if such Number be a Majority of the whole Number of Electors appointed; and if there be more than one who have such Majority, and have an equal Number of Votes, then the House of Representatives shall immediately choose by Ballot one of them for President; and if no Person have a Majority, then from the five highest on the List the said House shall in like Manner choose the President. But in choosing the President, the Votes shall be taken by States, the Representation from each State having one Vote; A quorum for this Purpose shall consist of a Member or Members from two thirds of the States, and a Majority of all the States shall be necessary to a Choice. In every Case, after the Choice of the President, the Person having the greatest Number of Votes of the Electors shall be the Vice President. But if there should remain two or more who have equal Votes, the Senate shall choose from them by Ballot the Vice President.

The Congress may determine the Time of choosing the Electors, and the Day on which they shall give their Votes, which Day shall be the same throughout the United States.

No Person except a natural born Citizen, or a Citizen of the United States, at the time of the Adoption of this Constitution, shall be eligible to the Office of President; neither shall any Person be eligible to that Office who shall not have attained to the Age of thirty five Years, and been fourteen Years a Resident within the United States.

In Case of the Removal of the President from Office, or of his Death, Resignation, or Inability to discharge the Powers and Duties of the said Office, the Same shall devolve on the Vice President, and the Congress may by Law provide for the Case of Removal, Death, Resignation or Inability, both of the President and Vice President, declaring what Officer shall then act as President, and such Officer shall act accordingly, until the Disability be removed, or a President shall be elected.

The President shall, at stated Times, receive for his Services, a Compensation, which shall neither be increased nor diminished during the Period for which he shall have been elected, and he shall not receive within that Period any other Emolument from the United States, or any of them.

Before he enter on the Execution of his Office, he shall take the following Oath or Affirmation:—"I do solemnly swear (or affirm) that I will faithfully execute the Office of President of the United States, and will to the best of my Ability, preserve, protect and defend the Constitution of the United States."

Section. 2

The President shall be Commander in Chief of the Army and Navy of the United States, and of the Militia of the several States, when called into the actual Service of the United States; he may require the Opinion, in writing, of the principal Officer in each of the executive Departments, upon any Subject relating to the Duties of their respective Offices, and he shall have Power to grant Reprieves and Pardons for Offences against the United States, except in Cases of Impeachment.

He shall have Power, by and with the Advice and Consent of the Senate, to make Treaties, provided two thirds of the Senators present concur; and he shall nominate, and by and with the Advice and Consent of the Senate, shall appoint Ambassadors, other public Ministers and Consuls, Judges of the supreme Court, and all other Officers of the United States, whose Appointments are not herein otherwise provided for, and which shall be established by Law: but the Congress may by Law vest the Appointment of such inferior Officers, as they think proper, in the President alone, in the Courts of Law, or in the Heads of Departments.

The President shall have Power to fill up all Vacancies that may happen during the Recess of the Senate, by granting Commissions which shall expire at the End of their next Session.

Section. 3

He shall from time to time give to the Congress Information of the State of the Union, and recommend to their Consideration such Measures as he shall judge necessary and expedient; he may, on extraordinary Occasions, convene both Houses, or either of them, and in Case of Disagreement between them, with Respect to the Time of Adjournment, he may adjourn them to such Time as he shall think proper; he shall receive Ambassadors and other public Ministers; he shall take Care that the Laws be faithfully executed, and shall Commission all the Officers of the United States.

Section. 4

The President, Vice President and all civil Officers of the United States, shall be removed from Office on Impeachment for, and Conviction of, Treason, Bribery, or other high Crimes and Misdemeanors.

Article III

Section. 1

The judicial Power of the United States shall be vested in one supreme Court, and in such inferior Courts as the Congress may from time to time ordain and establish. The Judges, both of the supreme and inferior Courts, shall hold their Offices during good Behaviour, and shall, at stated Times, receive for their Services, a Compensation, which shall not be diminished during their Continuance in Office.

Section. 2

The judicial Power shall extend to all Cases, in Law and Equity, arising under this Constitution, the Laws of the United States, and Treaties made, or which shall be made, under their Authority;—to all Cases affecting Ambassadors, other public Ministers and Consuls;—to all Cases of admiralty and maritime Jurisdiction;—to Controversies to which the United States shall be a Party;—to Controversies between two or more States;— between a State and Citizens of another State,— between Citizens of different States,—between Citizens of the same State claiming Lands under Grants of different States, and between a State, or the Citizens thereof, and foreign States, Citizens or Subjects.

In all Cases affecting Ambassadors, other public Ministers and Consuls, and those in which a State shall be Party, the supreme Court shall have original Jurisdiction. In all the other Cases before mentioned, the supreme Court shall have appellate Jurisdiction, both as to Law and Fact, with such Exceptions, and under such Regulations as the Congress shall make.

The Trial of all Crimes, except in Cases of Impeachment, shall be by Jury; and such Trial shall be held in the State where the said Crimes shall have been committed; but when not committed within any State, the Trial shall be at such Place or Places as the Congress may by Law have directed.

Section. 3

Treason against the United States shall consist only in levying War against them, or in adhering to their Enemies, giving them Aid and Comfort. No Person shall be convicted of Treason unless on the Testimony of two Witnesses to the same overt Act, or on Confession in open Court.

The Congress shall have Power to declare the Punishment of Treason, but no Attainder of Treason shall work Corruption of Blood, or Forfeiture except during the Life of the Person attainted.

U.S. Constitution

Article IV

Section. 1

Full Faith and Credit shall be given in each State to the public Acts, Records, and judicial Proceedings of every other State. And the Congress may by general Laws prescribe the Manner in which such Acts, Records and Proceedings shall be proved, and the Effect thereof.

Section. 2

The Citizens of each State shall be entitled to all Privileges and Immunities of Citizens in the several States.

A Person charged in any State with Treason, Felony, or other Crime, who shall flee from Justice, and be found in another State, shall on Demand of the executive Authority of the State from which he fled, be delivered up, to be removed to the State having Jurisdiction of the Crime.

No Person held to Service or Labour in one State, under the Laws thereof, escaping into another, shall, in Consequence of any Law or Regulation therein, be discharged from such Service or Labour, but shall be delivered up on Claim of the Party to whom such Service or Labour may be due.

Section. 3

New States may be admitted by the Congress into this Union; but no new State shall be formed or erected within the Jurisdiction of any other State; nor any State be formed by the Junction of two or more States, or Parts of States, without the Consent of the Legislatures of the States concerned as well as of the Congress.

The Congress shall have Power to dispose of and make all needful Rules and Regulations respecting the Territory or other Property belonging to the United States; and nothing in this Constitution shall be so construed as to Prejudice any Claims of the United States, or of any particular State.

Section. 4

The United States shall guarantee to every State in this Union a Republican Form of Government and shall protect each of them against

Invasion; and on Application of the Legislature, or of the Executive (when the Legislature cannot be convened), against domestic Violence.

Article V

The Congress, whenever two thirds of both Houses shall deem it necessary, shall propose Amendments to this Constitution, or, on the Application of the Legislatures of two thirds of the several States, shall call a Convention for proposing Amendments, which, in either Case, shall be valid to all Intents and Purposes, as Part of this Constitution, when ratified by the Legislatures of three fourths of the several States, or by Conventions in three fourths thereof, as the one or the other Mode of Ratification may be proposed by the Congress; Provided that no Amendment which may be made prior to the Year One thousand eight hundred and eight shall in any Manner affect the first and fourth Clauses in the Ninth Section of the first Article; and that no State, without its Consent, shall be deprived of its equal Suffrage in the Senate.

Article VI

All Debts contracted and Engagements entered into, before the Adoption of this Constitution, shall be as valid against the United States under this Constitution, as under the Confederation.

This Constitution, and the Laws of the United States which shall be made in Pursuance thereof; and all Treaties made, or which shall be made, under the Authority of the United States, shall be the supreme Law of the Land; and the Judges in every State shall be bound thereby, any Thing in the Constitution or Laws of any State to the Contrary notwithstanding.

The Senators and Representatives before mentioned, and the Members of the several State Legislatures, and all executive and judicial Officers, both of the United States and of the several States, shall be bound by Oath or Affirmation, to support this Constitution; but no religious Test shall ever be required as a Qualification to any Office or public Trust under the United States.

Article VII

The Ratification of the Conventions of nine States, shall be sufficient for the Establishment of this Constitution between the States so ratifying the Same.

DONE in Convention by the Unanimous Consent of the States present the Seventeenth Day of September in the Year of our Lord one thousand seven hundred and Eighty-seven and of the Independence of the United States of America the Twelfth. In WITNESS whereof We have hereunto subscribed our Names,

George Washington, President and deputy from Virginia

New Hampshire: John Langdon, Nicholas Gilman.

Massachusetts: Nathaniel Gorham, Rufus King.

Connecticut: Wm. Saml. Johnson, Roger Sherman.

New York: Alexander Hamilton.

New Jersey: Wil: Livingston, David Brearley, Wm. Paterson, Jona. Dayton.

Pennsylvania: B. Franklin, Robt. Morris, Tho: Fitzsimons, James Wilson, Thomas Mifflin, Geo. Clymer, Jared Ingersoll, Gouv: Morris

Delaware: George Read, John Dickinson, Jacob Broom, Gunning Bedford, Jun'r, Richard Bassett.

Maryland: James M'Henry, Danl Carroll, Dan: of St. Thos. Jenifer

Virginia: John Blair, James Madison, Jr.

North Carolina: Wm. Blount, Hu. Williamson, Rich'd Dobbs Spaight

South Carolina: J. Rutledge, Charles Pinckney, Charles Cotesworth Pinckney, Pierce Butler.

Georgia: William Few, Abr. Baldwin.

Attest, William Jackson, Secretary

THE BILL OF RIGHTS

Preamble

THE Conventions of a number of the States having at the time of their adopting the Constitution, expressed a desire, in order to prevent misconstruction or abuse of its powers, that further declaratory and restrictive clauses should be added: And as extending the ground of public confidence in the Government, will best insure the beneficent ends of its institution.

RESOLVED by the Senate and House of Representatives of the United States of America, in Congress assembled, two thirds of both Houses concurring, that the following Articles be proposed to the Legislatures of the several States, as Amendments to the Constitution of the United States, all or any of which Articles, when ratified by three fourths of the said Legislatures, to be valid to all intents and purposes, as part of the said Constitution; viz.:

ARTICLES in addition to, and Amendment of the Constitution of the United States of America, proposed by Congress, and ratified by the Legislatures of the several States, pursuant to the fifth Article of the original Constitution.

Amendment I

Congress shall make no law respecting an establishment of religion, or prohibiting the free exercise thereof; or abridging the freedom of speech, or of the press; or the right of the people peaceably to assemble, and to petition the Government for a redress of grievances.

Amendment II

A well-regulated Militia, being necessary to the security of a free State, the right of the people to keep and bear Arms, shall not be infringed.

Amendment III

No Soldier shall, in time of peace be quartered in any house, without the consent of the Owner, nor in time of war, but in a manner to be prescribed by law.

Amendment IV

The right of the people to be secure in their persons, houses, papers, and effects, against unreasonable searches and seizures, shall not be violated, and no Warrants shall issue, but upon probable cause, supported by Oath or affirmation, and particularly describing the place to be searched, and the persons or things to be seized.

Amendment V

No person shall be held to answer for a capital, or otherwise infamous crime, unless on a presentment or indictment of a Grand Jury, except in cases arising in the land or naval forces, or in the Militia, when in actual service in time of War or public danger; nor shall any person be subject for the same offence to be twice put in

jeopardy of life or limb; nor shall be compelled in any criminal case to be a witness against himself, nor be deprived of life, liberty, or property, without due process of law; nor shall private property be taken for public use, without just compensation.

Amendment VI

In all criminal prosecutions, the accused shall enjoy the right to a speedy and public trial, by an impartial jury of the State and district wherein the crime shall have been committed, which district shall have been previously ascertained by law, and to be informed of the nature and cause of the accusation; to be confronted with the witnesses against him; to have compulsory process for obtaining witnesses in his favor, and to have the Assistance of Counsel for his defence.

Amendment VII

In Suits at common law, where the value in controversy shall exceed twenty dollars, the right of trial by jury shall be preserved, and no fact tried by a jury, shall be otherwise re-examined in any Court of the United States, than according to the rules of the common law.

Amendment VIII

Excessive bail shall not be required, nor excessive fines imposed, nor cruel and unusual punishments inflicted.

Amendment IX

The enumeration in the Constitution, of certain rights, shall not be construed to deny or disparage others retained by the people.

Amendment X

The powers not delegated to the United States by the Constitution, nor prohibited by it to the States, are reserved to the States respectively, or to the people.

ADDITIONAL AMENDMENTS

Amendment XI

The Judicial power of the United States shall not be construed to extend to any suit in law or equity, commenced or prosecuted against one of the United States by Citizens of another State, or by Citizens or Subjects of any Foreign State.

Amendment XII

The Electors shall meet in their respective states and vote by ballot for President and Vice-President, one of whom, at least, shall not be an inhabitant of the same state with themselves; they shall name in their ballots the person voted for as President, and in distinct ballots the person voted for as Vice-President, and they shall make distinct lists of all persons voted for as President, and of all persons voted for as Vice-President, and of the number of votes for each, which lists they shall sign and certify, and transmit sealed to the seat of the government of the United States, directed to the President of the Senate;-The President of the Senate shall, in the presence of the Senate and House of Representatives, open all the certificates and the votes shall then be counted;-The person having the greatest Number of votes for President, shall be the President, if such number be a majority of the whole number of Electors appointed; and if no person have such majority, then from the persons having the highest numbers not exceeding three on the list of those voted for as President, the House of Representatives shall choose immediately, by ballot, the President. But in choosing the President, the votes shall be taken by states, the representation from each state having one vote; a quorum for this purpose shall consist of a member or members from two-thirds of the states, and a majority of all the states shall be necessary to a choice. And if the House of Representatives shall not choose a President whenever the right of choice shall devolve upon them, before the fourth day of March next following, then the Vice-President shall act as President, as in the case of the death or other constitutional disability of the President-The person having the greatest number of votes as Vice President, shall be the Vice-President, if such number be a majority of the whole number of Electors appointed, and if no person have a majority, then from the two highest numbers on the list, the Senate shall choose the Vice-President; a quorum for the purpose shall consist of two-thirds of the whole number of Senators, and a majority of the whole number shall be necessary to a choice. But no person constitutionally ineligible to the office of President shall be eligible to that of Vice-President of the United States.

Amendment XIII

Section 1

Neither slavery nor involuntary servitude, except as a punishment for crime whereof the party shall have been duly convicted, shall exist within the United States, or any place subject to their jurisdiction.

Section 2

Congress shall have power to enforce this article by appropriate legislation.

Amendment XIV

Section 1

All persons born or naturalized in the United States and subject to the jurisdiction thereof, are citizens of the United States and of the State wherein they reside. No State shall make or enforce any law which shall abridge the privileges or immunities of citizens of the United States; nor shall any State deprive any person of life, liberty, or property, without due process of law; nor deny to any person within its jurisdiction the equal protection of the laws.

Section 2

Representatives shall be apportioned among the several States according to their respective numbers, counting the whole number of persons in each State, excluding Indians not taxed. But when the right to vote at any election for the choice of electors for President and Vice President of the United States, Representatives in Congress, the Executive and Judicial officers of a State, or the members of the Legislature thereof, is denied to any of the male inhabitants of such State, being twenty-one years of age, and citizens of the United States, or in any way abridged, except for participation in rebellion, or other crime, the basis of representation therein shall be reduced in the proportion which the number of such male citizens shall bear to the whole number of male citizens twenty-one years of age in such State.

Section 3

No person shall be a Senator or Representative in Congress, or elector of President and Vice President, or hold any office, civil or military, under the United States, or under any State, who, having previously taken an oath, as a member of Congress, or as an officer of the United States, or as a member of any State legislature, or as an executive or judicial officer of any State, to support the Constitution of the United States, shall have engaged in insurrection or rebellion against the same, or given aid or comfort to the enemies thereof. But Congress may by a vote of two-thirds of each House, remove such disability.

Section 4

The validity of the public debt of the United States, authorized by law, including debts incurred for payment of pensions and bounties for services in suppressing insurrection or rebellion, shall not be questioned. But neither the United States nor any State shall assume or pay any debt or obligation incurred in aid of insurrection or rebellion against the United States, or any claim for the loss or emancipation of any slave; but all such debts, obligations and claims shall be held illegal and void.

Section 5

The Congress shall have power to enforce, by appropriate legislation, the provisions of this article.

Amendment XV

Section 1

The right of citizens of the United States to vote shall not be denied or abridged by the United States or by any State on account of race, color, or previous condition of servitude.

Section 2

The Congress shall have power to enforce this article by appropriate legislation.

Amendment XVI

The Congress shall have power to lay and collect taxes on incomes, from whatever source derived, without apportionment among the several States, and without regard to any census or enumeration.

Amendment XVII

The Senate of the United States shall be composed of two Senators from each State, elected by the people thereof, for six years; and each Senator shall have one vote. The electors in each State shall have the qualifications requisite for electors of the most numerous branch of the State legislatures.

When vacancies happen in the representation of any State in the Senate, the executive authority of such State shall issue writs of election to fill such vacancies: Provided, That the legislature of any State may empower the executive thereof to make temporary appointments until the people fill the vacancies by election as the legislature may direct.

This amendment shall not be so construed as to affect the election or term of any Senator chosen before it becomes valid as part of the Constitution.

Amendment XVIII

Section 1

After one year from the ratification of this article the manufacture, sale, or transportation of intoxicating

liquors within, the importation thereof into, or the exportation thereof from the United States and all territory subject to the jurisdiction thereof for beverage purposes is hereby prohibited.

Section 2

The Congress and the several States shall have concurrent power to enforce this article by appropriate legislation.

Section 3

This article shall be inoperative unless it shall have been ratified as an amendment to the Constitution by the legislatures of the several States, as provided in the Constitution, within seven years from the date of the submission hereof to the States by the Congress.

Amendment XIX

The right of citizens of the United States to vote shall not be denied or abridged by the United States or by any State on account of sex.

Congress shall have power to enforce this article by appropriate legislation.

Amendment XX

Section 1

The terms of the President and Vice President shall end at noon on the 20th day of January, and the terms of Senators and Representatives at noon on the 3d day of January, of the years in which such terms would have ended if this article had not been ratified; and the terms of their successors shall then begin.

Section 2

The Congress shall assemble at least once in every year, and such meeting shall begin at noon on the 3d day of January, unless they shall by law appoint a different day.

Section 3

If, at the time fixed for the beginning of the term of the President, the President elect shall have died, the Vice President elect shall become President. If a President shall not have been chosen before the time fixed for the beginning of his term, or if the President elect shall have failed to qualify, then the Vice President elect shall act as President until a President shall have qualified; and the Congress may by law provide for the case wherein neither a President elect nor a Vice President elect shall have qualified, declaring who shall then act as President, or the manner in which one who is to act shall be selected, and such person shall act accordingly until a President or Vice President shall have qualified.

Section 4

The Congress may by law provide for the case of the death of any of the persons from whom the House of Representatives may choose a President whenever the right of choice shall have devolved upon them, and for the case of the death of any of the persons from whom the Senate may choose a Vice President whenever the right of choice shall have devolved upon them.

Section 5

Sections 1 and 2 shall take effect on the 15th day of October following the ratification of this article.

Section 6

This article shall be inoperative unless it shall have been ratified as an amendment to the Constitution by the legislatures of three-fourths of the several States within seven years from the date of its submission.

Amendment XXI

Section 1

The eighteenth article of amendment to the Constitution of the United States is hereby repealed.

Section 2

The transportation or importation into any State, Territory, or possession of the United States for delivery or use therein of intoxicating liquors, in violation of the laws thereof, is hereby prohibited.

Section 3

This article shall be inoperative unless it shall have been ratified as an amendment to the Constitution by conventions in the several States, as provided in the Constitution, within seven years from the date of the submission hereof to the States by the Congress.

Amendment XXII

Section 1

No person shall be elected to the office of the President more than twice, and no person who has held the office of President, or acted as President, for more than two years of a term to which some other person was elected President shall be elected to the office of the President more than once. But this Article shall not apply to any person holding the office of President, when this Article was proposed by the Congress, and shall not prevent any person who may be holding the office of President, or acting as President, during the term within which this Article becomes operative from holding the office of President or acting as President during the remainder of such term.

Section 2

This article shall be inoperative unless it shall have been ratified as an amendment to the Constitution by the legislatures of three-fourths of the several States within seven years from the date of its submission to the States by the Congress.

Amendment XXIII

Section 1

The District constituting the seat of Government of the United States shall appoint in such manner as the Congress may direct:

A number of electors of President and Vice President equal to the whole number of Senators and Representatives in Congress to which the District would be entitled if it were a State, but in no event more than the least populous State; they shall be in addition to those appointed by the States, but they shall be considered, for the purposes of the election of President and Vice President, to be electors appointed by a State; and they shall meet in the District and perform such duties as provided by the twelfth article of amendment.

Section 2

The Congress shall have power to enforce this article by appropriate legislation.

Amendment XXIV

Section 1

The right of citizens of the United States to vote in any primary or other election for President or Vice President for electors for President or Vice President, or for Senator or Representative in Congress, shall not be denied or abridged by the United States or any State by reason of failure to pay any poll tax or other tax.

Section 2

The Congress shall have power to enforce this article by appropriate legislation.

U.S. Constitution

Amendment XXV

Section 1

In case of the removal of the President from office or of his death or resignation, the Vice President shall become President.

Section 2

Whenever there is a vacancy in the office of the Vice President, the President shall nominate a Vice President who shall take office upon confirmation by a majority vote of both Houses of Congress.

Section 3

Whenever the President transmits to the President pro tempore of the Senate and the Speaker of the House of Representatives his written declaration that he is unable to discharge the powers and duties of his office, and until he transmits to them a written declaration to the contrary, such powers and duties shall be discharged by the Vice President as Acting President.

Section 4

Whenever the Vice President and a majority of either the principal officers of the executive departments or of such other body as Congress may by law provide, transmit to the President pro tempore of the Senate and the Speaker of the House of Representatives their written declaration that the President is unable to discharge the powers and duties of his office, the Vice President shall immediately assume the powers and duties of the office as Acting President.

Thereafter, when the President transmits to the President pro tempore of the Senate and the Speaker of the House of Representatives his written declaration that no inability exists, he shall resume the powers and duties of his office unless the Vice President and a majority of either the principal officers of the executive department or of such other body as Congress may by law provide, transmit within four days to the President pro tempore of the Senate and the Speaker of the House of Representatives their written declaration that the President is unable to discharge the powers and duties of his office. Thereupon Congress shall decide the issue, assembling within forty-eight hours for that purpose if not in session. If the Congress, within twenty- one days after receipt of the latter written declaration, or, if Congress is not in session, within twenty-one days after Congress is required to assemble, determines by two-thirds vote of both Houses that the President is unable to discharge the powers and duties of his office, the Vice President shall continue to discharge the same as Acting President; otherwise, the President shall resume the powers and duties of his office.

Amendment XXVI

Section 1

The right of citizens of the United States, who are eighteen years of age or older, to vote shall not be denied or abridged by the United States or by any State on account of age.

Section 2

The Congress shall have power to enforce this article by appropriate legislation.

Amendment XXVII

No law varying the compensation for the services of the Senators and Representatives shall take effect, until an election of Representatives shall have intervened.

About the Author

Photo by Angie Moon

M. E. Boyd is an attorney with great interest in the United States Constitution and American history and philosophy. Miss Boyd was in private practice and taught business, educational, and Constitutional law as an adjunct professor. She also taught the U.S. Constitution for twelve years for a lifelong learning program. You may reach her at info@MissConstitution.com.

Notes

Part I

[i] John Jay, "Letter to the English Anti-Slave Society," *The U.S. Constitution: A Reader*, ed. Hillsdale College Politics Faculty. (Hillsdale: Hillsdale College Press, 2012), 409. Jay was one of the most important founders of America. He was close to George Washington and a chief negotiator for peace with Great Britain both at the end of the Revolution and in the subsequent early years of our nationhood. Jay was adamantly opposed to slavery. He was the first Chief Justice of the Supreme Court of the United States.

[ii] *Johnson and Graham's Lessee v. M'Intosh* (1823). This is one of Chief Justice John Marshall's most interesting cases involving private citizens purchasing land from native-Americans and a justification for "discovery" of lands already occupied by native-Americans.

[iii] The Articles of Confederation. The Articles of Confederation was our first national Constitution. See the Appendices.

[iv] John Dickinson, 1732-1808, had family homes in both Pennsylvania and Delaware. He does not have the same stature as other Founders, in part because he did not sign the Declaration of Independence. He was convinced that America was not sufficiently prepared to take on the British. One of his homes, Fairhill, was burned to the ground by the British in 1777. Fairhill was considered by some to be the most beautiful home in the colonies and the British deliberately targeted it for destruction. Dickinson was a quiet, thoughtful Quaker who carried himself with great dignity and had the respect of everyone who worked with him.

[v] Colin G. Calloway, *The Scratch of a Pen, 1763, and the Transformation of North America* (New York: Oxford University Press, 2006.) A wonderful story of how the British land holding in America more than doubled after the Seven Year's War in Europe and the French and Indian War in America. George Washington participated for the British and surrendered Fort Necessity in western Pennsylvania. The Fort is open to visitors today.

[vi] The United States Constitution. The United States Constitution is the first modern written constitution of its kind and scope. See the Appendices.

[vii] Washington, "Circular Letter to the States," 174-175. Commander in chief of the American forces against colonial Britain and first President of the United States. George Washington was a thoughtful and dignified person whose charisma was unparalleled. He considered himself an enlightened farmer. He had a fishing fleet and a distillery in addition to his farms. Washington's home, Mount Vernon, Virginia, close to Washington, DC, was left in ruins fifty years after his death. Congress refused to purchase Mount Vernon for the nation, and it was saved by a group of women who became the Mount Vernon Ladies Association. The Association still owns and runs the property. For character and moral rectitude there is no one who

compares to the Father of our Country. He was happily married to Martha Washington, though childless, and is buried at Mount Vernon. George Washington believed deeply in God but was not particularly religious. He was an ardent Freemason.

[viii] David O. Stewart, *The Summer of 1787* (New York: Simon & Schuster, 2007), 51.

[ix] Stewart, *The Summer of 1787, 111.*

[x] Paine, "Common Sense," 101 and 107. b.1737-d.1809. Thomas Paine was British by birth, He became a famous revolutionary pamphleteer later going to France during the French Revolution and imprisoned there. He was an avowed atheist.

[xi] *United States v. Seeger* (1965) granted conscientious objector status to a person having a sincere meaningful belief which occupies in that person's life a place parallel to that filled by an orthodox belief in God.

[xii] Patrick Henry, "Debates in the Virginia Ratifying Convention," *Annals of America,* 18 vols. ed. Mortimer J. Adler (Chicago: *Encyclopedia Britannica*, 1968), Vol 3, Selection 56. b.1736-d.1799. Henry is famous for his eloquent "Give Me Liberty or Give Me Death" speech in Virginia before the American Revolution. He was opposed to the ratification of the new Constitution. He believed it concentrated too much power in the federal government.

[xiii] Madison, "George Washington, John Adams, Benjamin Franklin, Alexander Hamilton, and James Madison on Slavery," 402. b.1751-d.1836. James Madison was the chief note-taker at the Constitutional Convention in 1787 in Philadelphia, PA. He was a Washington advisor. He became a supporter of Thomas Jefferson and was Secretary of State for both of his terms as President. He participated in the Louisiana Purchase which doubled the land mass of the United States. It was agreed by all who attended the Constitutional Convention that notes regarding negotiations and debate remain undisclosed until the last death of those that attended. There were no leaks and at Madison's death his extensive notes were finally revealed for historic research. He was the fourth President of the United States.

[xiv] James Jackson, quoted by Franklin, "Against The Slave Trade," *Annals,* Selection 84, 421-422. b.1757-d.1806. Jackson was born in Britain and emigrated to America as a teenager. James Jackson was elected Governor of Georgia but refused to serve because of inexperience. He was elected again a few years later and accepted the position. He was a defender of slavery and an opponent of the financial views of Alexander Hamilton.

[xv] Benjamin Franklin, "Against The Slave Trade," *Annals,* Vol. 3, Selection 84. b.1706-d.1790. Franklin was the most famous American of his day. He was best known as a scientist and ambassador to France when America needed French help to defeat the British in the American Revolution. A prolific writer, inventor and humorist his presence along with George Washington was critical in attracting the best American minds to the Constitutional Convention of 1787.

xvi Jefferson, "Notes on the State of Virginia Query XVIII: Manners," 404. b.1743-d.1826. Thomas Jefferson was perhaps the smartest politician America has produced. He was author of the Declaration of Independence as a member of a committee. He and John Adams were bitter political enemies though became friends late in life thanks, in part, to John's wife Abigail. They died on the same day (July 4). Jefferson was an early widower and classical scholar. He was third President of the United States and founder of the University of Virginia.

xvii Gustavus Vassa, "The Slave Ship," *Annals,* Vol. 3, Selection 114.

xviii Akhil Reed Amar, *America's Constitution: A Biography* (NY: Ransom House, 2005), 87-98.

xix Samuel Hopkins, "The Inconsistency of Slavery," *Annals,* Vol. 2, Selection 108. b.1721-d.1803. Hopkins was a Calvinist theologian and Congregational minister adamantly opposed to slavery in America.

xx The Declaration of Independence is the written reasons why America, as a colony of the British, fought a revolution to become an independent nation. The document gives very specific reasons and a philosophical overlay that represents natural law concepts that form one of the bundles of law that we are to obey as citizens of the United States and for any others within our jurisdiction. See the Appendices.

xxi John Dickinson. AZ Quotes.com, Wind and Fly LTD, 2019. https//www.AZQuotes.com/quote 570462, accessed February 14, 2019.

xxii William Cushing, "The Quock Walker Case: Slavery Unconstitutional in Massachusetts," *Annals,* Vol. 2, Selection146.

xxiii Abraham Lincoln, A Day of National Thanksgiving by the President of the United States of America: A Proclamation. Washington, DC, 1863. William Henry Seward may have written this for Lincoln. This Proclamation called for the day to be the last Thursday of November. It was changed to the fourth Thursday in November by Franklin Delano Roosevelt.

xxiv King James I, "First Charter of Virginia" *Essential Documents of American History: Volume 1,* ed. Bob Blaidsell, (Mineola, NY: Dover Publications, 2016), 3.

xxv Melancton Smith, "Changes Needed Before Ratifying the Constitution," *Annals,* Vol. 2, Selection 50. Smith was b.1744-d.1798. He opposed the ratification to the proposed Constitution in the New York ratifying convention.

xxvi *Barron v. Baltimore* (1833); the Supreme Court ruled that the Bill of Rights applies to federal government actors not state and local government actors. The Incorporation Doctrine displaced *Barron* for all but a few rights in the Bill of Rights that do not apply to the states. Each state has its own Constitution and civil rights were protected by state Constitutions not the federal Constitution. With the pass-through to states through the Due Process Clause of the 14th Amendment state actors are now subject to violations of federal civil rights. This fact has had tremendous impact on public schools that are considered state actors because they receive

---

taxpayer funds. At one time public schools were within the purview of the state but are now subject to additional challenges from the federal Constitution and federal mandates. The moral law was once thought important to impart to children in the public schools. It is founded on Judeo-Christian principles. The Incorporation Doctrine prevents much of this as a violation of the Establishment Clause of the 1st Amendment to the United States Constitution. Education itself is a right through state Constitutions not a fundamental right in the United States Constitution.

xxvii Hamilton, "Federalist 70," 345-351. Alexander Hamilton b.1757 d.1804. Hamilton is known as the founder of America's commercial economic system and one of the main authors of the Federalist Papers that supported ratification of the United States Constitution.

xxviii Amar, *America's Constitution,* Chapters. 4 and 5. This entire biography is an indispensable resource for every detail of the United States Constitution.

xxix Hamilton, "Federalist 78," 379-385.

xxx Alexis de Tocqueville, *Democracy in America*, eds. Mayer and Lerner (NY: Harper, 1966), 136-137. Alexis de Tocqueville was perhaps the greatest of all commentators on America. b.1805-d.1859. He travelled to America from France to study our penal institutions but was really interested in the elements that make America and Americans what they are. He was amazed at the earnestness and morality of the American people and felt that the invention of the township as a unit of local government was one of the great new ideas in governance because it kept all volatile issues local.

xxxi Gouverneur Morris, in a letter to John Dickinson, 1803. Gouverneur Morris b.1752-d.1816, is known as the penman of the Constitution. See the inspiring Preamble to the United States Constitution.

xxxii Credited to Benjamin Franklin.

Part II

xxxiii John Winthrop, "A Model of Christian Charity," *Annals,* Vol. 3, Selection 20. b.1588-d.1649. Winthrop was a Puritan, not a Separatist, but had a similar vision as William Bradford for the Massachusetts Bay Colony. The Colony received a royal patent and he brought many colonists in the large wave of emigrants in 1630. Massachusetts Bay Colony was wealthier and more prominent than Plymouth Colony, but both hoped for a utopian community that the Christian world could emulate. Separatists wanted to separate completely from the Anglican church of England; the Puritans wanted merely to purify it.

xxxiv Nathaniel Philbrick, *Mayflower* (New York: The Penguin Group, 2006), 4. This is a wonderful book full of rich history about the people and events surrounding the colonists north of Jamestown. For both the native-Americans and the arriving colonists, examples of virtuous, sincere, and wise persons abound. There are also others not so worthy. Equally excellent: Nick Bunker, *Making Haste From Babylon: The Mayflower Pilgrims and Their World* (New York: Alfred Knopf, 2010).

xxxv Philbrick, *Mayflower,* 5.

xxxvi Robinson, "Spiritual Advice to Pilgrim Planters," 61-64.

xxxvii Philbrick, *Mayflower,* 76.

xxxviii Bradford, "Of Plymouth Plantation," 65. b.1590-d.1657. Bradford came from a relatively well-to-do family in England but was orphaned early. He lived with uncles and came under the influence of a minister who was part of a reform movement to strip the Anglican church of its Catholic influences and was later imprisoned by authorities for his association with this movement. He and others went to Holland as weavers where they could worship as they pleased. The tight-knit group remained English and finally decided to leave Holland and its unhealthy conditions for the New World. William Bradford was a leader of great virtue and probity whose loyalty to Plymouth Colony was unconditional. He was one of the greatest of our early colonists.

xxxix Philbrick, *Mayflower,* 144-146.

xl Philbrick, *Mayflower,* 136.

xli Bernard Bailyn, *The Barbarous Years: The Conflict of Civilizations 1600-1665* (New York: Vintage Books, 2013), 100-107.

xlii Captain John Underhill, "Narrative of the Pequot War," *Essential Documents of American History: Volume I,* ed. Bob Blaisdell, (Mineola, NY: Dover Publications, 2016), 14.

xliii John Cotton, "Democracy as Detrimental to Church and State," *Annals,* Vol, 1, Selection 27. b.1585-d.1652. Cotton came from a distinguished background in England to Massachusetts Bay Colony as the most prominent Puritan scholar and theologian.

xliv In *Marsh v. Chambers* (1983), Justice Burger cites a quote from Justice William O. Douglas in a 1951 case, "[we] are a religious people whose institutions presuppose a Supreme Being." Our national motto was approved by Congress in 1956. Our national motto prior to that was *E Pluribus Unum,* or "from many, one" that is part of the Great Seal of the United States designed by Charles Thomson shortly after our nationhood was established.

xlv Massachusetts School Laws of April 14, 1642, and November 11, 1647," *Essential Documents,* 32.

xlvi S. Whitmore, *Bibliographical Sketch of the Laws of Massachusetts Colony* (1889), 32-60, online library of liberty, oll.libertyfund.org/pages/1641-mass-body-of-liberties.

xlvii The Flushing 'Remonstrance,' "Toleration for Quakers," *Annals,* Vol. 1, Selection 50.

[xlviii] James Madison, "Memorial and Remonstrance Against Religious Assessments," *The US Constitution: A Reader,* ed. Hillsdale College Politics Faculty. (Hillsdale: Hillsdale College Press, 2012), 129-134.

[xlix] Jefferson, "Virginia Statute for Religious Freedom," 135-136.

[li] *Barron v. Baltimore* (1833). This early case in our republic states that the Bill of Rights applies only to the federal and not state governments. The Incorporation Doctrine is a modern construct of the Supreme Court, especially Justices Black and Frankfurter, and was not applied in any impactful way until 1962 and *Engel v. Vitale* (1962) that prohibited prayer in public schools. No case save *Roe v. Wade* (1973) has had more impact on our society than this case as it altered traditional educational practice relative to teaching character and humility to children. One of the premises in this and later cases is that children should not be coerced into religious views as children are not mature enough to make critical judgments and distinctions for themselves. This would be true of political-view coercion as well and the basis for the Hatch Act on the federal level and little Hatch Acts on the state level restricting some political activity by state actors such as public school teachers in promoting their personal political opinions to students who do not have the maturity to critically assess. It should be remembered that each state has its own constitution and the Founders envisioned states deciding for themselves through their own governing documents about "establishing" religion in their state. This deference to state power was an important component of the thinking in the Constitutional Convention of 1787 and is known as Federalism.

[lii] Madison, "Federalist 51," 287-291.

[liii] This is the prayer that was what was at issue in the now famous *Engel v. Vitale* (1962) case that ended the practice of prayer in public schools. "Almighty God, we acknowledge our dependence upon Thee, and we beg Thy blessings upon us, our parents, our teachers and our Country." This prayer was recommended by the State Board of Regents, an agency created by the New York State Constitution with supervisory powers over public education in New York. Prayer in private schools is not banned as private schools are not arms of the state, or state actors, to which the Bill of Rights applies.

[liv] Alexis De Tocqueville, *Democracy in America,* ed. Richard D. Heffner, (New York: Signet Classic, 2001), 48.

[lv] George Hoar, "The Lust for Empire," *Annals,* Vol. 12, Selection 57. Senator from Massachusetts and a leading anti-imperialist.

[lvi] Elizabeth Cady Stanton, "The Natural Rights of Civilized Women," *Annals,* Vol. 9, Selection 28.

[lvii] Some of the excellent leadership includes Frederick Douglass, Senator Blanche Bruce, and Booker T. Washington. In an 1886 speech Douglass says, "Though we

have had war, reconstruction, and abolition as a nation, we still linger in the shadow and blight of an extinct institution. Though the colored man is no longer bought and sold, he is still surrounded by an adverse sentiment which fetters all his movements."

lviii Walter Hines Page, "The Significance of the War with Spain," *Annals,* Vol. 12, Selection 42.

lix James Bradley, *The Imperial Cruise* (New York: Little Brown, 2009), 48. "Teddy absorbed a scholarly, reasoned case for American world domination based upon the color of his skin and thus had acquired the prism through which he would judge people, events, and nations." Bradley's source: Thomas G. Dyer, *Theodore Roosevelt and The Idea of Race,* 5.

lx Albert J. Beveridge, "The Taste of Empire," *Annals,* Vol. 12, Selection 43.

lxi James Bradley, *The Imperial Cruise,* 79. "[t]he Atlantic Constitution ridiculed McKinley as a 'goody-goody man,' calling for a declaration of American virility . . . At this moment there is a great need of a man in the White House . . .the people need a man – and American – at the helm. . . Roosevelt remarked to a friend, 'McKinley has no more backbone than a chocolate éclair.'" Bradley's source: Edmund Morris, *The Rise of Theodore Roosevelt.* 555.

lxii William McKinley, "War Message," *Annals,* Vol. 12, Selection 40. McKinley was the 25th President. He was assassinated in 1901 just months after his re-election. Teddy Roosevelt became President and began his secret negotiations in Asia regarding the Japanese, the Russians, the Koreans, and the Chinese. He greatly favored the Japanese and agreed to a secret treaty with them that allowed the Japanese to subjugate the Koreans.

lxiii James Bradley, *The Imperial Cruise,* 106. "Typically, when the U.S. Army arrived, soldiers rounded up the mayor, town officials, priests, and any other potential sources of information. 'Water detail' an officer would bark, and up came the torturers with their black tools. In the Philippines conflict waterboarding was known as the water cure." Bradley's source: Richard Drinnon, *Facing West: The Metaphysics of Indian-Hating and Empire Building,* 320.

lxiv July 4, 1946.

lxv Thomas B. Reed, "Empire Can Wait," *Annals,* Vol.12, Selection 36. One of the ablest Speakers of the House in America's history and a master parliamentarian.

lxvi Charles Eliot Norton, "The Desertion of Ideals," *Annals,* Vol. 12, Selection 71. Norton was a well-regarded professor at Harvard and felt America could never recover from her venture into imperialism and empire building.

lxvii James Bradley, *The Imperial Cruise,* 156. In 1893 the U.S. Minister to Hawaii gave the order for the *coup d'etat* that deposed the Hawaiian Queen.

lxviii Doris Kearns Goodwin, *The Bully Pulpit* (New York: Simon & Schuster, 2013), 427. In 1903 President Roosevelt sent ships to support Panamanians against Columbia and quickly negotiated a deal to purchase land for a canal. "I took the Canal Zone,"

Roosevelt boasted. Roosevelt also secretly involved himself in the Sino-Russian conflict on behalf of Japan for which he won the Nobel Peace Prize as "neutral."

[lxix] Jerome Barron and C. Thomas Dienes, *Constitutional Law In A Nutshell* (St, Paul, MN: West Publishing, 2005), 27 and 28. *Marbury v. Madison* (1803) established the notion of judicial review of the constitutionality of acts of Congress.

[lxx] George Washington, "Farewell Address," *The U.S. Constitution: A Reader,* ed. Hillsdale College Politics Faculty, (Hillsdale College Press, 2012), 149-150.

[lxxi] Jack London, "How I Became A Socialist," *Annals,* Vol. 13, Selection 11.

[lxxii] *Dictionary of Philosophy and Religion,* 3rd ed., s.v. "Marxism." Karl Marx b.1818–d.1883, a German economist and philosopher wrote *The Communist Manifesto* with Friedrich Engels in 1847. Among other things he believed that the conflict between capitalists and proletarians would be world-wide. With the triumph of the working class, it would eventually be followed by a classless society.

[lxxiii] Henry David Thoreau, "Resistance To Civil Government," *Annals,* Vol. 7, Selection 117.

[lxxiv] Bailyn, *The Barbarous Years,* 311-322.

[lxxv] Barbara Tuchman, *The Proud Tower* (New York: Random House, 2014), Chap. 2.

[lxxvi] Tuchman, *Proud Tower,* 95.

[lxxvii] Women's Christian Temperance Union, Declaration of Principles," *Essential Documents of American History: Vol. II,* 75.

[lxxviii] De Tocqueville, *Democracy,* 247.

[lxxix] *Dictionary of Philosophy and Religion,* "Nihilism." Nothing exists; nothing can be known; if it were known it could not be communicated. "Vienna Circle of Logical Positivists" If it can't be scientifically proven it does not exist. Many of its members moved to the United States from Germany during Hitler's regime and went to major universities where they had a huge impact on American higher education. Among other things the Vienna School wanted to eliminate metaphysics as pseudo-propositional. "Metaphysics" Metaphysics is the study of being and is considered the first philosophy by Aristotle. For Thomas Aquinas it is the study of transcendent being or the being of God himself. Many ideations, coming from European philosophers in the 19th and early 20th century, were atheistic or extremely skeptical with both Nietzsche and Sartre believing God to be dead and Sartre believing that nothingness is equivalent to being. See also the Frankfurt School and its reinterpretation of Marxism. All these variations of the extremely negative and pessimistic counter the philosophical foundations of the American system which considers a belief in God essential and adherence to them would negate natural and moral law precepts which are at the heart of our Rule of Law. The American experiment can be summed up as organizing principles that assume a Supreme Being without mandating that the individual citizen believe it in his or her personal life. What is essential to the structure may nevertheless be denied by those benefitting

from that structure- the ultimate irony. In the statecraft of the world never has such an attempt been made to enshrine freedom of conscience into law for individual people.

Part III

lxxx "Statutes of William and Mary," *Annals of America,* Vol. 1, Selection 87.

lxxxi "Massachusetts School Laws of April 14, 1642 and November 11, 1647," *Essential Documents: Vol.1,* p. 32.

lxxxii Plymouth Colony School Laws," *Annals,* Vol. 1, Selection 55.

lxxxiii "On Parental Duty and the Apprenticeship of Children," *Annals,* Vol. 1, Selection 33.

lxxxiv *San Antonio Independent School District v. Rodriguez* (1973). Justice Powell: "Education is not among the rights afforded explicit protection under our Federal Constitution."

lxxxv Charles Woodmason, "Lawlessness on the South Carolina Frontier," *Annals,* Vol. 2, Selection 39.

lxxxvi *Pierce v. Society of Sisters* (1925). Justice McReynolds in one of the most important Supreme Court cases in our history writes, "The fundamental theory of liberty upon which all governments in this Union repose excludes any general power of the State to standardize its children by forcing them to accept instruction from public teachers only. The child is not the mere creature of the State; those who nurture him and direct his destiny have the right, coupled with the high duty, to recognize and prepare him for additional obligations."

lxxxvii Francis W. Parker, "Salvation on Earth Through Education," *Annals,* Vol. 12, Selection 47.

lxxxviii John Dewey, "The School and Social Progress," *Annals,* Vol. 12, Selection 59.

lxxxix John L. Spalding, "Religion as an Essential Part of Education," *Annals,* Vol. 12, Selection 17.

xc Mary Antin, "The Promise of Free Education," *Annals,* Vol. 13, Selection 66.

xci Aaron Copland, "The Composer in Industrial America," *Annals,* Vol. 17, Selection 38.

xcii Sinclair Lewis, "The American Fear of Literature," *Annals,* Vol. 15, Selection 14.

xciii *Cohen v. California* (1971). Speech must be protected even if offensive. Justice Harlan, "One man's vulgarity is another's lyric."

xciv Mary Harris "Mother" Jones, "Appeal to the Cause of Miners in the Paint Creek District," *Essential Documents: Vol II,* p. 107.

xcv W.E.B. DuBois, "Credo," *Essential Documents: Vol. II,* p. 77.

xcvi Helen Hunt Jackson, "The Indian and the White Man," *Annals,* Vol. 10, Selection 107.

[xcvii] Marcus Garvey, "The Handwriting is on the Wall," *Essentials,* p. 131.

[xcviii] Will Rogers, "The Normal Majority," *Annals,* Vol. 14, Selection 89.

[xcix] Arthur Herman, *How the Scots Invented the Modern World* (New York: Broadway Books, 2001). This book's value in its entirety regarding the Scottish Enlightenment and its contributions to our thinking and our system cannot be exaggerated.

[c] Upton Sinclair, "The Meat Packers of Chicago," *Annals,* Vol. 13, Selection 17.

[ci] Chinese Exclusion Act," *Annals,* Vol. 10, Selection 112.

[cii] Jane Addams, "Industrial Amelioration and Social Ethics," *Annals,* Vol. 12, Selection 103.

Conclusion

[ciii] Simone de Beauvoir. "Goodbye to America," Vol. 16. Selection 110.

[civ] Yoram Hazony, "The Dark Side of the Enlightenment," *Wall Street Journal,* April 7-8, 2019, A, 11.

[cv] Thomas L. Friedman, "The Two Codes Your Kids Need to Know," *New York Times,* February 12, 2019, Opinion.

[cvi] Marcus Tullius Cicero, "On the Commonwealth," in James E. G. Zetzel, ed. *On the Commonwealth and On the Laws* (Cambridge: Cambridge University Press, 1999), 71-72.

[cvii] Address before Young Men's Lyceum of Springfield, IL 1838.

Made in the USA
Las Vegas, NV
30 April 2022

48212519R00143